A WORLD BY ITSELF

A World by Itself

THE PASTORAL MOMENT
IN COOPER'S FICTION

H. Daniel Peck

New Haven and London   Yale University Press

1977

Published with assistance from
The Louis Stern Memorial Fund.

Designed by John O. C. McCrillis
and set in Baskerville type.
Printed in the United States of America by
The Vail-Ballou Press, Inc., Binghamton, N.Y.

Published in Great Britain, Europe, Africa, and Asia
(except Japan) by Yale University Press, Ltd.,
London. Distributed in Latin America by Kaiman &
Polon, Inc., New York City; in Australia and New
Zealand by Book & Film Services, Artarmon, N.S.W.,
Australia; and in Japan by Harper & Row,
Publishers, Tokyo Office.

Library of Congress Cataloging in Publication Data

Peck, H   Daniel.
   A world by itself.

   Bibliography: p.
   Includes index.
   1.   Cooper, James Fenimore, 1789-1851—Criticism and
interpretation.   I.   Title.
PS1438.P4   813'.2   76-25868
ISBN 0-300-02027-9

To my mother and in memory of my father

Contents

Preface

Mark Twain's catalogue of literary offenses still has its admirers, a fact which reminds us of the risks we take when we defend the art of James Fenimore Cooper. Although many readers find Cooper's novels compelling, they are often hard pressed to locate the source of his power. And in the absence of a convincing explanation, critics have generally emphasized the writer's historical rather than literary significance. Cooper, it is said, stands at the beginning of American fiction, and his major contribution is a series of important innovations. He has been credited with inventing modern sea fiction, the western, the international novel, and with first giving literary treatment to tensions and themes that later writers were to develop more fully. His fiction, in other words, has been made to serve primarily as an example of tendencies in American thought and art, and it isn't surprising that some of the most interesting investigations of his work have come from cultural critics and historians.

Cooper was a deeply concerned observer of society, and his writings are an important source for the study of Jacksonian America. In *Fenimore Cooper: Critic of His Times*, Robert Spiller effectively initiated the form of criticism that concentrates upon the novelist's social thought. Since the publication of Spiller's biography in 1931, this emphasis has been strong and steady, as the recent appearance of John P. McWilliams's *Political Justice in a Republic* confirms. The interest in Cooper's role as a social critic has been salutary; it has given to several of his late and long-ignored novels the attention they deserve, and it has clarified our understanding of his political thought. But it has also resulted in some overemphases and distortions. Although Cooper's writings serve nicely as an example of a certain kind of response to social change, I do not think a reading of his work sustains Spiller's judgment that his was the "most thoroughly critical mind that early America produced" (317). Although he is astute at times, much of his social commentary is personalized and literalistic. I find it hard to disagree with Marvin Meyers's conclusion, in *The Jacksonian Persuasion*, that "Fenimore Cooper, reconsidered as a social critic, does not emerge with unsuspected qualities of originality, profundity, or subtlety" (57). Yet, despite these limitations, many literary critics have given almost exclusive attention to Cooper's social thought.

Cooper has been put to a related use by Henry Nash Smith, R. W. B. Lewis, Edwin Fussell, and others who have found in his writings one of the dominant myths of our culture—that of the "virgin land." Studies dealing with the American historical consciousness have demonstrated the significance of Cooper's literary response to the wilderness. But such examinations do not focus upon the unique qualities of the writer's fiction so much as they show how his work exemplifies widespread cultural assumptions. Their objective, which lies far beyond Cooper himself, is to discover in the novels support for historical theory. This is meant in no way to diminish the importance of these studies; it is merely to point out that they necessarily treat Cooper's landscapes as a function of attitudes toward the frontier, rather than as elements in an imaginative world. When, for example, Lewis writes of the "hero in space," a concept he applies to Leatherstocking, he is referring not so much to aesthetic space as to a mythologic/historical context.

More purely aesthetic responses to Cooper's landscapes have come from novelists such as Balzac and Lawrence; we are all familiar with the latter's exclamation in *Studies in Classic American Literature*: "Pictures! Some of the loveliest, most glamorous pictures in all literature" (55). And, in recent years, scholars too have become interested in the specifically visual aspects of the writer's work. James F. Beard, Donald A. Ringe, and Howard Mumford Jones have found that Cooper's narrative descriptions obey many of the same conventions as do the paintings of Thomas Cole and other Hudson River School artists. One full-length study, by James T. Callow, shows that these men were close associates who influenced each other deeply, who were indeed "kindred spirits." And recently a book by Ringe has appeared which deals historically and analytically with the pictorialism of Cooper, Bryant, and Irving. Works like these* are important because they help us to see Cooper in the context of the dominant modes of his time and in terms of the artistic intentions he saw for himself.

Understandably, however, studies of this kind deal principally with classification and analysis; they enumerate the tallying points between the visual and literary arts and explain the systems of aesthetics that stand behind these analogies. Such examinations tell us how eighteenth-century landscape conventions of the beautiful, the picturesque, and the sublime inform Cooper's fiction, and how prevailing attitudes concerning the passage of time and the power of nature influenced his art. But because the object of these investigations is to delineate and match categories, they fail to render the dynamics of Cooper's space *as* space. Ultimately, they do not tell us why a particular novel continues to move us.

Studies of Cooper's pictorialism, then, are as unsatisfactory as examinations of his social thought and historical consciousness. All of these tend to hold his fiction at a distance, to place it rather than engage its imaginative qualities directly. They provide us with standard interpretations which control our responses to the novels and circumscribe the field of inquiry. For example, Cooper's works are often defined exclusively by the familiar polarity, civilization versus nature. But to read a romance like *The Deerslayer*, with all its complex and mysterious appeal, is to recognize the limits of such categories. We need a more flexible and responsive criticism, one which takes fuller

*Cited in my bibliography. Also see Blake Nevius's monograph, *Cooper's Landscapes*, which appeared too late for me to incorporate its useful findings in this book. For an excellent bibliographic review of the various forms of Cooper criticism summarized above, see James F. Beard's contribution to *Fifteen American Authors before 1900*.

account of the writer's literary power. As Lawrence perceived, Cooper "was truly [and foremost] an artist" and only secondarily "an American" and "a gentleman" (48). For too long, attention has been focused on these secondary roles, and in this study I have attempted to address the artist.

Acknowledgments

I owe most to Sherman Paul, who prepared me to undertake this project and gave to it warm encouragement and incisive criticism. Of special importance to me is the way in which Professor Paul invited my own style of exploration, and taught me to trust my discoveries. This is a large debt, of which learning and method are only parts, and these few words are but a gesture toward repayment.

There are several others whose help I have greatly valued. Alan Trachtenberg gave the manuscript a good, hard reading which moved me to a fuller and clearer argument. I was fortunate, indeed, to have Ellen Graham of the Yale University Press as my editor; she identified for me the real structure of my book. David Thorburn made a large contribution of encouragement and support.

It pleases me to thank my colleagues, Peter Carafiol, Herbert Schneidau, and Fred See, each of whom read the entire manuscript and made many valuable suggestions. At every stage of this project's development, Kent Dixon has given me indispensable help with the writing. John Gerber, W. R. Irwin, and Alexander Kern offered perceptive readings of an early version. And Mimi Dixon and Jody Millward provided expert editorial assistance.

I would also like to thank William Frost and Frank Gardiner for their administrative courtesy and support, and to acknowledge the University of California, Santa Barbara, and the University's Academic Senate Committee on Research, for providing a summer fellowship and research funds which enabled me to complete my revisions.

Needless to say, I am indebted to many who have worked on Cooper before, but especially to James F. Beard, whose call for a specifically literary response to the novels I have attempted—however successfully—to answer.

This is my opportunity to thank Nathan Lyons for first stimulating my interest in American literature, and Matthew Coughlin for many years of loyal friendship. Ruth Peck receives the last and most important place in these acknowledgments. Despite the demands of her own career, she has provided a structure in which to work and has been one of my best and most enthusiastic readers.

H.D.P.

Santa Barbara

PART I

The Language of the Eye

As Wilder bent his look again on this growing object, the Rover put a glass into his hands, with an expression which the other understood to say, "You may perceive that the carelessness of your dependent has betrayed us!" Still the look was one rather of regret than of reproach; nor did a single syllable of the tongue confirm the language of the eye.

The Red Rover

1

The Primacy of the Image

Some might insist on speaking of symbol, allegory, metaphor, and ask the philosopher to designate moral lessons before images. But if images were not an integral part of moral thought, they would not have such life, such continuity.

Gaston Bachelard, *L'air et les songes*

James Fenimore Cooper confessed in a letter of 1823 his "antipathies" to Thomas Jefferson. "I was brought up in that school," he explained, "where his image seldom appeared, unless it was clad in red breeches, and where it was always associated with the idea of infidelity and political heresy." The occasion was a visit to a library which housed a Thomas Sully portrait of the former president. Noting that he "would have gone twice as far to see the picture of almost any other man," Cooper went on to describe the surprise and even shock of seeing this portrait for the first time: "There was a dignity, a repose, I will go further, and say a loveliness, about this painting, that I never have seen in any other portrait." The important thing for Cooper, however, was not the loveliness itself but the dramatic transformation it worked on him: "In short I saw nothing but Jefferson, standing before me, not in red breeches and slovenly attire, but a gentleman, appearing in all republican simplicity, with a grace and ease on the canvas, that to me seemed unrivalled."

Somehow, Cooper was certain, the portrait had revealed to him the essence of Jefferson's character, and in doing so had displaced a previous conception: "it has really shaken my opin-

ion of Jefferson as a man, if not as a politician; and when his
image occurs to me now, it is in the simple robes of Sully, sans
red breeches, or even without any of the repulsive accompaniments of a political 'sans culotte.' "[1] Although Cooper's subsequent examination of Jefferson's writings led him to a fuller
appreciation,[2] his original reevaluation came in this sudden
and momentary witnessing of a portrait.

The remarkable conversion recorded in the letter communicates the great power of the visual in Cooper's imagination. When he writes that the portrait "has *really* shaken my
opinion" (my italics), I think we should read "really" not as an
intensifier for "shaken" (as in modern usage), but to mean
literally that the transformation is real, substantive, even permanent. His use of the word "image" suggests not just a pictorial representation but a total configuration of Jefferson the
man, a complex idea of which the visual is an integral and
controlling element. The "red breeches" that Cooper had previously associated with Jefferson, for example, are not merely
symbolic of "political heresy." Rather, the two terms seem to be
virtually interchangeable, with the image and the idea bearing
a different and closer relationship than symbol-for-thing.

The language of the letter describes a mental process in
which one "image," a complete, discrete entity, has been ex-
changed for another; Jefferson in "red breeches and slovenly
attire" has been replaced by Jefferson in "the simple robes of
Sully." And, most remarkable of all, this experience leads
Cooper to feel that he has recognized or discovered (not inter-
preted) the final and true "image" of Thomas Jefferson's
character. His response indicates a faith in immediate visual

1. *The Letters and Journals of James Fenimore Cooper*, ed. James F. Beard, 1:
95–96. Hereafter this edition of Cooper's correspondence will be referred to
as *L&J*.

2. Writing to Charles Wilkes (from Rome) in April of 1830, Cooper asks:
"What do you think of Jefferson's letters? Have we not had a false idea of that
man? I own he begins to appear to me, to be the greatest man, we ever had"
(*L&J*, 1:411). For a political interpretation of this conversion, see John P.
McWilliams, Jr., *Political Justice in a Republic*, pp. 44–46.

perception which distinguishes his sensibility from our own and also from that of several other great writers of nineteenth-century American romanticism.

Cooper's literalistic faith in the veracity and reliability of the visual image can be accounted for, in part, by referring to the intellectual background of his age. In the most general way, his understanding of the relation of perceiver to perceived is Lockean. For Cooper, as for Locke, the question of correspondence between "ideas" in the mind and "reality" is not seriously problematical. The world and its reflected images in human consciousness do not exist across a chasm of darkness and uncertainty, but in a relatively stable and verifiable relationship. This distinctly eighteenth-century confidence in the reliability of perception and the orderliness of the universe certainly helps to explain Cooper's sensibility.

But more directly relevant is the influence, pervasive in early nineteenth-century America, of the Scottish Common Sense philosophers—such thinkers as Thomas Reid, Dugald Stewart, and Archibald Alison. The effect these philosophers had on American writers has been explored elsewhere, and it would not be useful to rehearse those findings at length here. But it should be noted that the realism and empiricism promulgated by this school had great appeal to Americans, many of whom were anxious to refute philosophical skepticism and to assert the reliability of the senses.

Common Sense thought carried another important implication, however; for while the senses are trustworthy, they are also capable of exciting in us certain qualities of mind through the power of association. Thus a landscape can, under favorable circumstances, engender a sense of nobleness of purpose, or of the benevolence of God. And if objects of the natural landscape have this evocative power, then objects of art do also. In fact, Alison and others of this school argued, landscape paintings have greater power than natural landscape because their creators can screen out the superfluous and represent only those aspects of the natural world certain to create meaningful associations.

But even more evocative than visual art is the art of poetry, which has far greater range and subtlety. As Alison formulates it, "The painter can represent no other qualities of nature, but those which we discern by the sense of sight. The poet can blend with those, all the qualities which we perceive by means of our other senses."[3] Still, if the poet can fill out his conception of nature with the "other senses," for him too sight remains dominant. Post-Lockean aesthetic theory implies a strong link between the idea and the *visual* image. As Ernest Tuveson has written, "Since ideas are images, since even complex ideas are multiple pictures, and since understanding itself is a form of perception, the visual and the intellectual would tend to become amalgamated."[4]

This strong visual emphasis clearly informs Cooper's sense of narrative. The moment of conception of many of his novels seems to have occurred with the viewing of a natural scene, a scene either witnessed accidentally (Susan Fenimore Cooper said that a sudden glimpse of Lake Otsego through the forest inspired her father to write *The Deerslayer*) or deliberately sought out for inspiration.[5] Several of the novels, such as *The Oak Openings* and *The Prairie*, celebrate a landscape in their titles, and others, like *The Pioneers* and *The Pathfinder*, refer to the setting in their subtitles (*The Sources of the Susquehanna* and *The Inland Sea*, respectively). *The Deerslayer* finally took a subtitle emphasizing human action (*The First War-Path*), but earlier the writer had preferred one (*A Legend of the Glimmerglass*) which focuses upon the landscape (*L&J*, 4:112). This and

3. Cited by Donald A. Ringe, *The Pictorial Mode,* p. 7. For this brief summary of the influence of Common Sense philosophy on the thought of Cooper's time, I am indebted to Ringe's book, cited here, to William Charvat, *The Origins of American Critical Thought: 1810–1835,* and to Terence Martin, *The Instructed Vision.*

4. *The Imagination as a Means of Grace,* p. 73.

5. See Susan Fenimore Cooper's remarks in *Pages and Pictures,* pp. 322–23. In 1832, from Switzerland, Cooper wrote Samuel F. B. Morse that he was about "to go on the Great St. Bernard with Mr. Cox. We shall see if the mountain cannot be worked up in the way of a romance" (*L&J*, 2:337).

other similar cases[6] suggest that Cooper thought of narrative more in terms of scene than character. He once planned, in fact, to write a sea novel which would contain no human characters (*L&J*, 4:162). In all of his works, large portions of the narrative are given over to natural description.

In itself, the visual quality of Cooper's fiction does not distinguish it from that of several other writers of his age (consider, for example, the pictorialism of Sir Walter Scott and Maria Edgeworth). But there are indications that he placed even greater importance on the specifically visual aspects of experience than did most of his contemporaries. As his response to the Sully portrait suggests, Cooper believed that in some direct and immediate way the human eye perceives, or is capable of perceiving, the "truth." This belief helps to explain his great concern for visual accuracy in narrative description. Although many historical novelists of his time, especially American writers, felt "the urge to be a realist,"[7] Cooper's was an unusually literalistic imagination. Modern readers, who are especially aware of his official rhetoric and dependence on convention, may wonder at his claims for realism, yet Cooper's desire for visual accuracy is unmistakable. We know, for example, that he was critical of Scott's sea novel, *The Pirate*, because he felt it did not render accurate images of the nautical life. Cooper made it clear that he wrote his own first romance of the sea, *The Pilot*, for the specific purpose of correcting Scott's errors.[8] His objections to *The Pirate* may sound simpleminded as literary criti-

6. For example, *The Hutted Knoll* became the subtitle of *Wyandotté* (a character's name), but Cooper originally intended the former phrase as the main title. See *L&J*, 4:380, 382, 388.

7. See Harold C. Martin, "The Development of Style in Nineteenth-Century American Fiction," in *Style in Prose Fiction*, p. 121. For a discussion of how Cooper's prefaces reveal his sense of himself as a realist, see Arvid Shulenberger, *Cooper's Theory of Fiction*. Also see Cooper's *Early Critical Essays: 1820–1822*, ed. James F. Beard.

8. See Cooper's second preface to *The Pilot*, published originally in the 1831 English edition, and published in slightly revised form in the 1849 Putnam edition.

cism, but they indicate how important visual accuracy was to him.

Cooper's travel journals reveal still another aspect of his literalistic imagination—an intense faith in the validity and vitality of first impressions. He loved scenery, and his reports of walking tours on the European continent tell of his utter rapture over unexpected vistas. He tended to cling to the images of such scenes, to hold them tightly, as it were, so that he might possess them forever in his imagination. Returning to places he had first toured a year or two earlier, he often expresses disappointment at their failure to evoke again what he calls "extasies with the country." As he observes in one of his journals, "With me, the effect of a second look is generally to diminish the impression." In a journal entry of 1832, describing his return to a Swiss chapel, Cooper tells his reaction: "The view from the chapel is very pretty, but not as fine as I had pictured it from recollection. The first time I came upon [it?] by surprise, and perhaps I now expected too much."[9] This naive delight in first impressions, combined with a sophisticated artistic sensibility, is one of the defining characteristics of Cooper's imagination. He possessed a peculiarly focused and concentrated intelligence which riveted itself to the image and clung to it with unswerving tenacity.

This same quality of mind can be detected in every area of Cooper's concern. For example, his image of America, almost pictorial in a certain way, was so tightly structured that when he was confronted with the realities of Jacksonian democracy after seven years in Europe, he began an insistent argument with his country which he sustained for the rest of his life. The nature of his response suggests that he would not, perhaps could not, depart from his initial conception.

9. For the quotations, see *L&J*, 2:386, 299, 319. Cooper's travel books contain many such references to the value of surprise. In *Sketches of Switzerland*, pt. 1, vol. 1, he tells of entering a beautiful valley for the first time: "The effect of this sudden transition on us all, was like that of passing into a new world" (36). Two pages later, he reveals his disappointment at entering the next valley, even more beautiful than the one referred to above, but which does not take him "so completely by surprise" (38).

In the present context, however, it is not so important to insist upon Cooper's peculiarly literalistic imagination, or to understand the philosophical foundation for his response to the image, as it is to discover how this response actually informs his fiction and makes it unique and even powerful. What must concern us at present is how the image functions in Cooper's imagination and, conversely, how it does not.

Marius Bewley sees Cooper standing "at or near the beginning of the symbolist tradition in American fiction—that tradition by which the American artist was able to overcome, in a handful of great books, the impoverishment of his social milieu." Regarding Leatherstocking as "a beautifully realized symbol," Bewley places Cooper's novels in close relation to those of Hawthorne and Melville and criticizes Charles Feidelson, Jr., for not treating them in *Symbolism and American Literature*.[10] But Feidelson was correct in his omission, because Leatherstocking and Lake Glimmerglass are not symbols in the same sense as are the Scarlet Letter and Moby Dick; and to associate Cooper too closely with mid-nineteenth-century romantic symbolism is to miss the real source of his power.

The distinction I wish to introduce here concerns the function and effect of the visual image in Cooper's work as compared with the symbolic imagery of writers such as Melville and Hawthorne. In the work of these latter novelists, the image, as I have developed the term, tends to be ambiguous, multivalent, essentially mysterious, and carries its meaning (or significant lack of meaning) to the private soul. For Ahab, the white whale bears one cluster of meanings, for Ishmael another, and for Starbuck still another—but the final and ultimate meaning remains hidden. For these writers, the images of the natural world are merely symbolic of a deeper (and darker) reality. As Frederick Crews has written of Hawthorne, "Good Romantic that he was, he located reality squarely in the buried life of the

10. *The Eccentric Design*, pp. 20, 101–12, 311n. Cf. Leslie Fiedler on Cooper's development outside the influence of New England Calvinism, and the lack of "residual secular Puritanism" in his thought (*Love and Death in the American Novel*, pp. 184–85).

mind."[11] But Cooper is not a romantic in this sense, and for him the visual is never the "mere" visual. As we have seen, the image for him was capable of carrying the full weight of meaning immediately, without contradiction or ambiguity.

Although it is common in discussions of *The Deerslayer* to refer to Lake Glimmerglass as a beautiful "symbol" of the pristine wilderness (that is, of the *idea* of an unspoiled nature), the relationship between the Glimmerglass and nature is really more synecdochical than symbolic. While Moby Dick (for Ahab at least) symbolizes a metaphysical truth which lies deeper than the deceptive "pasteboard mask" of reality, the Glimmerglass might better be said to condense or epitomize the immediately recognizable beauties of the physical world. Unlike Hawthorne's dark, morally ambiguous forest and Melville's unfathomable ocean (or consider Poe's mysterious land and seascapes), the "truth" of the Glimmerglass is open to human understanding.[12]

Cooper's response to the visual image is closer to that of Transcendentalists like Emerson and Thoreau, who have confidence in the substantiality and reliability of nature. The epistemological and moral status of Walden Pond, for example, is not ambiguous; its spirituality is clear. The image of the Pond is as "real" for Thoreau as the Glimmerglass is for Cooper. Yet it is also true that Walden Pond has a symbolic dimension the Glimmerglass lacks. We would not expect Cooper to say, as Thoreau says in *Walden*, "I am thankful that this pond was made deep and pure for a symbol" (287). Because his sensibility is preromantic, he does not share

11. *The Sins of the Fathers*, p. 270. The distinction I am making can be emphasized by noting Cooper's important part in the early nineteenth-century celebration of American landscape that found expression in Bryant's poetry, Cooper's and Irving's prose, and paintings of the Hudson River School artists. This celebratory attitude contrasts with Hawthorne's characteristic distrust of nature. See Roderick Nash, *Wilderness and the American Mind*, chaps. 3 and 4.

12. Even Cooper's unpredictable and destructive ocean, in the sea tales, is not "unfathomable" in the Melvillean sense. Rather, it is defined by readily identifiable descriptive norms such as "sublimity."

Thoreau's desire to find "within" the natural world a deeper meaning.[13] That is to say, he is not troubled or intrigued by the ways of consciousness as such, and feels no need to discover a "correspondence" between the world of mind and the world of matter. The relationship between the image and its meaning in Cooper tends much more toward "equivalence" than toward symbolic "correspondence."

Walden Pond is a *deep* body of water, charged with the mystery of spiritual exploration, a symbol of the world of mind and an aspect of the Emersonian Not-me which takes on primary importance as it becomes interfused with the Me. The Glimmerglass, on the other hand, is imaginatively evocative for Cooper precisely because it is so clearly "other." As we shall see, Cooper must hold nature at a distance because it is the unfailing constant by which he is able to measure the inevitable failings of men. Unlike Transcendental versions of nature, in which the landscape has both objective and subjective meaning, the natural world in Cooper's fiction does not answer back (co-respond). The Glimmerglass, for example, does not emit the "sounds" of Walden. Rather, it offers itself as a silent model for moral instruction. It cannot merge with the world of consciousness, for then it would lose its purely objective (and therefore moral) status.

Nevertheless, in spite of its lack of symbolic import, the image of the Glimmerglass has touched many readers' imaginations profoundly. Cooper's most compelling visual images resonate with an intensity suggestive of the power of symbolism but somehow different in quality. The work of Gaston Bachelard can help us make this distinction, for in *The Poetics of Space* Bachelard defines what may be called a primary image, an image which prompts the feeling of a "poetic power rising naively within us" before more complex associations begin to

13. Unlike Melville, who wants to see "through" (beyond or "behind") nature to the hidden depths, Thoreau locates spirit within nature. He never leaves the phenomenal world behind even as it becomes symbolic for him. For this and several other observations on Thoreau in the following discussion of symbolism, I am indebted to Sherman Paul.

form. "After the original reverberation," Bachelard writes, "we are able to experience resonances, sentimental repercussions, reminders of our past" (xix). A writer like Thoreau deepens and fills out this original reverberation with the substance of his inner reality (the Real Self); Cooper, unconcerned with a distinction between inner and outer realities, fixes his attention on the world. He responds intensely to those resonant primary images within himself, but instead of putting them to symbolic "use," he simply allows them a privileged space in his imagination. Lacking the metaphysical yearning characteristic of both Thoreau and Melville,[14] Cooper sees things in nature *as things*; for him the natural world is defined objectively and communicates its meaning as "value" rather than as "symbol." Yet because the image of the Glimmerglass *glimmers* with such great intensity, because in Heidegger's phrase it "shines out," it communicates a vital force, or presence, which reminds us of symbolism but does not require transcendent validation. Cooper's reality, in other words, can be said to be immanent. While Thoreau must perform an act of mind to make Walden fully resonant (suggesting the importance for the symbolist writer of perception, "seeing-into"),[15] Cooper seems simply to *discover* the beauty of the Glimmerglass. This essentially innocent, even childlike, response to the visual image is responsible, I think, for much of the writer's appeal.

The Glimmerglass communicates its power through the radiance of its surface rather than as a function of its depth. We may remember that the lake is shallow at its center, where Thomas Hutter has secured Muskrat Castle on a shoal. Walden, on the other hand, is deepest at the center, as it must be

14. Although Cooper may be "the most religious of our major novelists," his religion is, as Charles A. Brady admits, of the "orthodox" kind ("Myth-Maker and Christian Romancer," p. 64). His historical vision is secular rather than theological (see Edgar A. Dryden, "History and Progress," p. 58 and passim), and religion seems to have served him principally as a solace in his later years, and as a psychological defense against change (see my discussion in part 4).

15. See chap. 2 for the difference between Emerson's and Cooper's understanding of the function of sight.

because it is a symbol of the self. And while the surface of Walden is often "ruffled"—it only becomes glassy when Thoreau is in perfect spiritual accord with it—the Glimmerglass is consistently imaged as a mirror. Though constant in its seasonal rhythms, Walden is variegated, circulating, changeful (sometimes the changes—the "circulations of being"—replace mirroring as Thoreau's primary symbolic motion). But the Glimmerglass is always perfectly still, a "mirrorlike surface" of "deep repose."[16]

It is interesting to notice that while the imagery of fishing— the quality of abundant, swimming life beneath the surface— intensifies the value of Walden Pond, we do not think of the Glimmerglass as a body of water to be fished, as if the presence of organic life would taint its purity, its precariously balanced, classic beauty. Unlike Walden, the Glimmerglass is not "seemingly bottomless" (189), nor do we wish that it were. Its magic is its reverberating reflectiveness, a quality which does not invite self-exploration so much as it induces reverie. There is a kind of (psychological) depth in this response, but it is not the symbolic depth suggested by Thoreau's plumbing the bottom of Walden Pond.

All of this will concern us more directly in the chapters that follow. At this point it is sufficient to stress that Cooper differs both from dark romantics such as Melville, Hawthorne, and Poe, who regard the world's surface as illusory, ambiguous, even duplicitous, and from Transcendentalists like Emerson and Thoreau, who have confidence in their relation to the physical world but find in this relation a symbolic correspondence. The visual appropriation of nature's truth in Cooper's

16. James Fenimore Cooper, *The Deerslayer; or, The First War-Path,* Darley-Townscend edition (New York, 1859–61), pp. 33, 45. Hereafter all citations of Cooper's novels will be from this edition, and the page references will follow the quotations in parentheses. In the few cases in which the source of the quotation is not identified in my discussion, an abbreviated form of the title will accompany the page reference. In those cases, the following abbreviations have been used: *The Deerslayer, D; The Last of the Mohicans, LM; The Oak Openings, OO; The Red Rover, RR; The Water Witch, WW; The Wept of Wish-ton-Wish, W.*

work is not complex or problematical, as it often is for symbolist writers for whom truth has become an individual (subjective, private) affair of experience. When his characters gaze at
a distant scene, they find in the landscape those values that
reflect an eighteenth-century predisposition to see in nature
certain clearly defined "associations": the benevolence and
power of God, the orderliness of the universe, sublimity, and
the inevitability of cosmic justice—truths that are not private or
enigmatic but public and apparent.

Cooper not only trusts the world's surface; he insists upon its
sufficiency and transparency. In the preface to one of his late
works, *The Oak Openings*, he repeats sentiments he had enunciated often throughout his long career: "It ought to be matter
of surprise how men live in the midst of marvels, without
taking heed of their existence." "Thus," he continues, "is it ever
with men. The wonders of creation meet them at every turn,
without awakening reflection, while their minds labor on subjects that are not only ephemeral and illusory, but which never
attain an elevation higher than that the most sordid interests
can bestow" (v–vi). In Cooper's view, all that is required of man
is his attention.

Although I have argued that Cooper is not a symbolist, it
would be misleading to say that he never uses symbols or that
he is unconcerned with certain kinds of conflict between appearance and reality. For example, he often deals with mistaken identity and moral paradox. In his work, however, such
problems are posed (and resolved) in secular rather than
metaphysical terms. As John Lynen has shown, Cooper's reality is a constant. Neither his setting nor his characters really
evolve; instead, his narratives develop by revealing gradually
what has always been true,[17] and the truths revealed are
human and comprehensible. The characters (and the reader)
may be temporarily confused, but this is not because of an
essential ambiguity at the heart of existence. Rather, Cooper

17. *The Design of the Present,* pp. 178–80 and passim.

has simply (for the moment) denied us a full view of the novel's "picture"; once it is viewed, all ambiguities dissolve.

Even when Cooper employs gothic effects and deliberately introduces seeming discrepancies between the apparent and the real, these effects do not produce the profound uncertainties characteristic of genuine gothic fiction, such as that of Poe and Brockden Brown. In Cooper's world, there is usually very little "slippage" between reality and states of mind. He takes great care to resolve a novel's apparent contradictions, often simultaneously in a discovery scene and, like Scott, almost always does so with natural rather than supernatural explanation.[18] We rarely are left with even the slightest lingering ambiguity.

Cooper, of course, can be a deliberate symbol-maker, sometimes for the purposes of allegory. In *The Sea Lions*, for example, he sets two ships on parallel Antarctic journeys to symbolize contrasting ways of life. *The Heidenmauer* features two prominent hills which represent the twin powers of church and state in ancient Germany. In *The Bravo*, the dark and labyrinthine corridors of the city-state of Venice symbolize political corruption. *The Monikins* is a political allegory set in the mythical kingdoms of Leaphigh and Leaplow. And the island setting of *The Crater* is an obvious symbol of America; the novel allegorizes the nation's social development.

Cooper specialists have attempted, in recent years, to convince us that this symbolic use of setting is skillful. One, for example, analyzes *The Headsman* to show how the writer "consciously sought appropriate symbolic representation of his ideas."[19] But these scholars have been preoccupied with demonstrating that Cooper was a more deliberate and careful writer than has generally been acknowledged, and in making their case they may have overvalued effects which in them-

18. In a significant exception, *The Water Witch*, Cooper allows certain magical phenomena to remain unexplained, but the effect is lyrical rather than gothic. See Yvor Winters, "Fenimore Cooper, or The Ruins of Time," pp. 196–98. Also see my discussion of *Lionel Lincoln*, pp. 107–08.

19. Donald A. Ringe, *James Fenimore Cooper*, p. 67.

selves have little appeal. It does not seem to me that Cooper's allegorical use of space distinguishes his work from that of numerous other writers, many of whom employ their symbols more skillfully (and subtly) than he. And even if this were not true, I think we sometimes wish Cooper's "ideas" themselves were more attractive or were, at least, communicated less dogmatically. For all the stunning Antarctic scenery depicted in *The Sea Lions*, the novel is seriously marred by the insistent argument for Trinitarianism that intrudes at every stage of the narrative. And it is no accident that the works most obviously employing a symbolic geography for didactic purposes are seldom read today. This is not merely a case of an author's inability to "stay out" of his work (*The Deerslayer* contains much authorial commentary and moral lesson, yet somehow we do not mind). For Cooper seems to have called upon allegory at just those times when his urge to tell, rather than show, was most intense. Thus, many parts of *The Crater*, a novel which served the writer as a kind of weapon, inevitably read like argumentation. And when modern readers find power in Cooper's fiction, I doubt that it is this Cooper who moves them.

If we are to define the qualities that distinguish Cooper's landscapes from those of other writers, I think we must turn to D. H. Lawrence's incomplete but suggestive reading of the Leatherstocking tales in *Studies in Classic American Literature*. Lawrence was angered by Cooper's pretensions as a professional author and knew that his strengths were not those of the deliberate craftsman. He maintained that the writer, almost in spite of himself, had produced a "lovely myth" (60), a myth that was compelling because it moved the reader to suspend belief from the realities of the American environment and character. Lawrence said that Natty Bumppo and Lake Glimmerglass were cases of pure fantasy, "wish-fulfillment" (49), and that Cooper's deepest desire was to *be* Natty and to inhabit the magic space of the American woods.

Perhaps Lawrence was able to direct our attention toward the real sources of Cooper's power because he felt free to admit that his response to the writer's "marvelously beautiful" scenes might be "childish" (55). When he wrote of the "exquisite" (60) beauty of the Glimmerglass, he approached Cooper's imagery not as symbolism or allegory but as an expression of what Bachelard calls "youthful language." Defending his phenomenological study of literary space, Bachelard asks that we "study poetic images in their exalting reality." "The image, in its simplicity," he argues, "has no need of scholarship. It is the property of a naive consciousness."[20]

With Cooper it could never be quite that simple; matters of pictorial and aesthetic convention weigh too heavily to be ignored completely, and an understanding of his perceptive process is necessary. But Bachelard's emphasis is salutary; he moves us in the right direction if we are to come to terms with the power of the writer's work. And in our attempt to follow the flow of images that fill and order the space of Cooper's novels, we must consider his fiction as an imaginative world with structures, tensions, and resonances of its own.

20. *The Poetics of Space*, pp. xxvii and xv.

2

The Eye of the Pilot

"When the danger is great, it is my gift to see it, and know it, and to try to avoid it; else would my scalp, long since, have been drying in a Mingo wigwam."

The Pathfinder

When Cooper wrote in *The Pilot* that his purpose was "solely to treat of man, and this fair scene on which he acts, and that not in his subtleties, and metaphysical contradictions, but in his palpable nature" (105), he was asserting that he was not a visionary writer. Yet modern criticism has sometimes insisted on making him one. Richard Poirier's study of American literary style, *A World Elsewhere*, is an example of such tendencies. Poirier has given us an exciting and important analysis of American writers' attempts to find satisfactory forms of expression (to build "a world elsewhere" through style). But his argument is so ranging that it necessarily shows signs of stress in its treatment of individual authors. The point of greatest strain may be the placement of Cooper in a continuum defined by American writers' belief in "the integrity and at least momentary autonomy of visionary experience" (63). American literature is characterized, according to this thesis, by protagonists who establish a "relation to landscape . . . by gazing at it, by an 'aesthetic contemplation' rather than by more palpable and profitable claims to ownership" (61).

In Poirier's view, Deerslayer becomes "still another version of Emerson's poet" (73), in that both figures seek a visionary possession of America and American space. It should be advanced immediately that Cooper's relation to his character is very different from Emerson's relation to his poet. Whereas

18

the poet obviously speaks for his creator's own mode of appropriating nature, Deerslayer does not represent Cooper's most basic response to landscape; that response is much better characterized by the narrator of *The Chainbearer*: "I examined the view with the interest which ownership is apt to create in us all. The earth is very beautiful in itself; but it is most beautiful in the eye of those who have the largest stake in it" (126). For Cooper, "palpable" possession is inextricably related to aesthetic contemplation, an attitude which hardly corresponds with Emerson's. My concern at this point, however, is not the difference between ways of possessing the landscape[1] but a distinction between the *processes* of perceiving the world. As we shall see, there are two distinct visual modes in Cooper's fiction, neither of which is visionary.

Emerson's famous passage in *Nature* on the "transparent eyeball" provides Poirier with the text for his argument, and I shall examine it briefly in order to show how it demonstrates not so much a continuity as a discontinuity between the "vision" of Cooper and Emerson:

> The charming landscape which I saw this morning, is indubitably made up of some twenty or thirty farms. Miller owns this field, Locke that, and Manning the woodland beyond. But none of them owns the landscape. There is a property in the horizon which no man has but he whose eye can integrate all the parts, that is, the poet. This is the best part of these men's farms, yet to this their warranty-deeds give no title. . . .
> . . . In the woods, we return to reason and faith. There I feel that nothing can befal me in life,—no disgrace, no calamity, (leaving me my eyes,) which nature cannot repair. Standing on the bare ground,—my head bathed by the blithe air, and uplifted into infinite space,—all mean egotism vanishes. I become a transparent eye-ball. I am nothing. I see all. The currents of the Universal Being circulate through me; I am part or particle of God. [9, 10]

1. For the relation of sight to possession, see my discussion in chap. 11.

These passages show that for Emerson the eye possesses a power to integrate the elements of the landscape into a vision-ary whole. Lockean dualism is overcome in the electric mo-ment of perception, in which self and world, matter and spirit, are united.[2] The objects of sight cease to register only as Mil-ler's field or Manning's, but coalesce into "Nature." Individual elements within the landscape serve symbolically as the trans-cendent is seen through the phenomenal.

The phrase, "I become a transparent eyeball," reveals much about the quality and motion of Emerson's seeing. The word "transparent" suggests that the poet's whole being (and his state-of-being) is filled with light. By shifting the emphasis to the word "become," we recognize that the eye is not an agent of the self in the moment of transcendence; rather, the self transmutes into a complete perceptual organ. Vision is not an independent power directed by the will, as in older faculty psychologies, but is synonymous for an instant with the self, as "the currents of the Universal Being circulate through [it]." The direction of the flow of power is inward, a drawing in of images through the filtering and integrating capacity of the self. In this way, the quality of Emersonian vision is more passive (eastern) than active-aggressive (western). The trans-parent eyeball does not penetrate space linearly or unidirec-tionally; instead, the landscape forms a circle around it, and the nature of perceptual acquisition suggests absorption rather than probing, sensitivity and openness rather than acuity or focusing.

The vision that characterizes Deerslayer and Cooper's other heroes really has little in common with such transcendent seeing. It is true that Leatherstocking is capable of a profound aesthetic appreciation of the landscape, and this will concern us shortly. But it is also true that such appreciative vision does not distinguish him from many other figures in Cooper's fiction—especially women characters—who share this capacity with him. The vision that distinguishes the hero in Cooper's work is of a more aggressive and practical kind, vision which

2. See Sherman Paul, *Emerson's Angle of Vision*, esp. chap. 3.

can isolate an enemy's presence within a mass of foliage or detect a nearly invisible imprint in the grass. These are the kinds of (nonmetaphysical) tasks that Leatherstocking's "accurate and fastidious eye" (*LM*, 261) performs. In *The Last of the Mohicans*, Uncas declares, " 'We call him Hawk-eye . . . for his sight never fails' " (394), and in *The Pioneers*, the older Natty Bumppo recalls that " 'the Indians named me for my sight' " (321).

When a Cooper hero focuses his eyes upon the natural world for the purpose of piloting a ship or pathfinding, he performs a visual task distinguishable from that of heroes of nineteenth-century symbolist literature, literature with a close philosophical relation to Emerson's thought. In *Moby Dick*, for example, Ahab searches the sky for nothing less than "objects on the unknown, thither side of . . . [the] sun" (412), and the hero of *Walden* complains that "our vision does not penetrate the surface of things" (96). Both these figures wish to probe regions beyond the visible phenomena of the world (although first they must thoroughly see, and comprehend, nature at the phenomenal level), and their heroism is associated with this visionary desire. But Cooper's heroes are characterized by their ability to read carefully, sometimes painstakingly, what is open for all to see but can in fact be isolated only by the "practised eye." That is, they are distinguished by the power of *observation* rather than by the power of *interpretation*. And although Leatherstocking's visual skill helps to give him mythic stature, this does not obviate the fact that the Cooper hero is a see-er, not a seer.[3] His heroism is defined by a special acuity of those senses we all possess, principally the eye but also the ear.

Sherman Paul has written that the vision of Emerson's poet can be analogized with "distant vision," as it is defined by Ortega y Gasset.[4] Ortega says that distant vision occurs when we no longer focus upon an object in the foreground but "let

3. Cf. Margaret Fuller on "the pilot-minds of the age" (*Papers on Literature and Art*, p. 331) and Coleridge's distinction between Imagination and Fancy. Also see F. O. Matthiessen on the symbolic function of sight in nineteenth-century thought (*American Renaissance*, pp. xiv, 44–55).

4. Paul, pp. 75–79.

the eye, passive but free, prolong its line of vision to the limit of the visual field." When this happens, "Nothing possesses a sharp profile." Instead, "the duality of proximate vision is succeeded by a perfect unity of the whole visual field." The sight for which the Indians have named Hawkeye is not distant vision but its opposite, "proximate vision." Where the former mode "synthesizes, combines, throws together," Ortega says that proximate vision "dissociates, analyzes, distinguishes." With "tactile" force, the "eye-beam" projects itself aggressively outward into space to strike the contours of an object or person; it "organizes the whole field of vision, imposing upon it an optical hierarchy: a privileged central nucleus articulates itself against the surrounding area."[5] In Cooper's fiction, proximate vision becomes heroic seeing.

The best example of the focusing and analyzing visual power of Cooper's heroes is to be found in *The Pilot*, for John Paul Jones is a character whose heroism is defined almost exclusively by his ability to *see*. The novel is set on the coastal waters off Great Britain during the revolutionary war, and in the ocean setting the eye has special, even vital, functions. In the more enveloping and textured environment of the woods, the other senses, particularly hearing, must be keen. But the pilot of a ship depends almost entirely upon the eye.

Unlike the transparent eyeball, which becomes nearly synonymous with the self (seeing as a way of being), the "eye of the Pilot" is represented as a quasi-independent agency directed by, but not an integral part of, the self: "The eye of the Pilot examined this armament closely" (100). Like a weapon, it is often described as an accessory, as part of the equipment of heroism. John Paul Jones directs his eye-beam outward into the murky coastal atmosphere to probe the near and the far for phenomena that have importance to navigation. At times, he appears to possess telescopic perception: "[He] glanced his eyes along the range of coast, as if he would ascertain the exact position of the vessel, and then turned them on the sea and the western horizon to scan the weather" (476).

5. José Ortega y Gasset, "On Point of View in the Arts," pp. 824, 831. Cf. Rudolf Arnheim, *Art and Visual Perception*, p. 28.

Heroic vision in Cooper is not a raw power. It is always used in conjunction with an exact and ranging knowledge of the setting. This combination defines the "instructed" or "practised" eye, and in his role as "guide" (37) the Pilot employs instructed vision for the same purposes as does Natty Bumppo when he leads a party through the wilderness. (In Cooper's forest novels, experienced pathfinders are sometimes referred to as pilots.) Just as Pathfinder is infinitely knowledgeable concerning his own "sea," the American forest, the Pilot (a native of the territory of the novel's setting) possesses complete knowledge of the British coastline waters. At one point, he is questioned about the dangers of navigation, and his answer establishes the relationship between seeing and knowing: " 'much, very much of my early life was passed on this dreaded coast. What to you is all darkness and gloom, to me is as light as if a noon-day sun shone upon it' "(55).

In *The Last of the Mohicans*, Hawkeye remarks, " 'Providence has lent to those who inhabit the woods eyes that would be needless to men in the settlements, where there are inventions to assist the sight' " (266). Throughout that novel, the "acuteness [of perception] which distinguished [Leatherstocking]" (259) is contrasted with Duncan Heyward's dependence on "rules" and "bookish knowledge." Similarly, the skill and great powers of observation that characterize John Paul Jones contrast with the relative ineptitude and inexperience of the genteel hero of *The Pilot*, Hugh Griffith. As Cooper describes it, this is a difference between the power of immediate perception and reliance upon abstract reckoning. When neither "time, lead nor log" (44) will serve, the Pilot dispenses with all tools of navigation and relies entirely upon the instructed eye. At one such moment, when the American crew is overcome by fear and confusion because of an approaching storm, the captain orders his first officer to " 'yield the trumpet to Mr. Grey [the Pilot's alias]; he alone can save us' " (58). And in the climactic sea chase of the novel, John Paul Jones guides his ship through dangerous shoals at great speed in a desperate attempt to evade the British forces. In this scene, Cooper offers the fullest example of the instructed eye (the "beacon") working in con-

junction with the commands of the voice (the "trumpet"): "The
Pilot jumped on a gun, and bending to catch a glimpse through
the smoke, he shouted, in those clear, piercing tones, that
could be even heard among the roaring of the cannon" (461).
Like Hawkeye in *The Last of the Mohicans*, the Pilot rises to the
occasion of leadership when conventional military authorities
have lost control.

This is as far as we can go, however, in identifying the Pilot
with Leatherstocking. Although both figures are, in one sense,
subversives,[6] John Paul Jones is to be distinguished from the
pure and simple Natty Bumppo because of his passion and
restlessness, qualities which Cooper must ultimately condemn.
Like Captain Heidegger of *The Red Rover*, the Pilot is modeled
after the Noble Outlaw developed by Byron and Scott.[7] Appropriately, his passionate inner life is revealed most fully by
his eyes: "The scornful expression that kindled the eye of the
Pilot, like a gleam of sunshine lighting for an instant some dark
dell and laying bare its secrets, was soon lost in the usually quiet
look of his glance, though he hesitated like one who was
struggling with his passions" (442).

The Pilot's vision is not only acute and probing; it is also
aggressive and destructive: "The Pilot fastened his glowing
eyes on him" (394). And like the Satanic Captain Heidegger,
his vision projects itself with an implicitly sexual force. These
qualities link him to gothic villains of eighteenth-century fiction (figures from whom the Noble Outlaw derived),[8] whose
eyes are always depicted as "penetrating" and threatening.
John Paul Jones reminds us of Schedoni in Ann Radcliffe's *The
Italian*, who possesses eyes "so piercing that they seemed to

6. For an interesting discussion of Leatherstocking's derivation from the
romantic outlaw, see John Seelye, "Some Green Thoughts on a Green Theme,"
pp. 596–99.

7. For a discussion of the Noble Outlaw in Byron and Scott, see Peter L.
Thorslev, Jr., *The Byronic Hero*, esp. chap. 5. For the Byronic characteristics of
Cooper's Rover, see Thomas Philbrick, *James Fenimore Cooper and the Develop-
ment of American Sea Fiction*, pp. 61–62.

8. For this development and a treatment of the gothic villain, see
Thorslev, chaps. 3 and 4.

penetrate, at a single glance, into the hearts of men, and to read their most secret thoughts" (1: 69–70).

Although Cooper regarded the Noble Outlaw as an exciting and attractive figure, he could never identify fully with a character whose eyes "flash with a terrible fire" (393). The Pilot's deep and ineradicable flaw is willful pride; he is motivated not by selfless idealism but by "wild ambition" (421). A clear indication of his self-absorption is the fact that he never pauses to admire a land or seascape, which is to say that he has no true concern with the outer world. His only relation to that world is established by his probing, analytical vision; in this sense, he is *unifocal.* Although he sometimes gives himself to contemplation, his look of "desperate and still calmness" (177) at such moments tells us that the object of his contemplation is the "dark dell" of his own turbulent soul. By looking only inward, he denies himself the "enlightening" moral instruction that nature offers freely to those who look outward.

The Pilot's vision is of the kind that Gaston Bachelard, in his study of poetic reverie, dismisses as irrelevant: "the aggressiveness of the *penetrating* look is of no concern." The " 'bad eye,' " as Bachelard calls it, is directed "against men" and "against things." "More contemplative, less aggressive" seeing, he writes, makes possible "our admiration of the world." While the Pilot lacks the capacity to admire the world, Leatherstocking has it within him to become the poet-dreamer. In *The Deerslayer*, we find him "gazing at the view [of the Glimmerglass] which so much delighted him," a view which gives him "that soothing of the spirit which is a common attendant of a scene so thoroughly pervaded by the holy calm of nature" (45). "Gentleness of seeing while admiring"—this is what Bachelard calls the experience that Leatherstocking feels as "pure delight," a sensation which proves he is "not insensible to the innate loveliness of such a landscape." Deerslayer feels, Cooper tells us, "like a poet also" (45).

It is appropriate and important that while the Pilot's environment is the tempestuous ocean, Deerslayer is the admirer of a lake. For as Bachelard says, in the presence of "still water,

the dreamer *adheres* to the repose of the world." "Dreaming
before . . . [still] water, one knows a sort of stable reverie," an
experience which gives the viewer the feeling that the "universe has lost all functions of *against.*"[9] Later, we will investigate the antipodal relation between Cooper's imaginative
ocean and lake, but for now we need only stress that Leatherstocking, unlike the Pilot, has the capacity to engage in *both*
heroic and contemplative seeing.

It is true, of course, that in the other Leatherstocking tales,
Natty Bumppo is not so admirative of nature as he is in *The
Deerslayer.* Yet in none of the tales—not even in *The Last of the
Mohicans*, where his responses are least poetic—does his analytical, probing vision become Byronic and destructive. For
Leatherstocking's heroic eyesight is disassociated—perhaps
abstracted—from those Byronic attributes that characterize
the vision of John Paul Jones. There is no veiled licentiousness
or repressed hatred in his gaze. Instead, his visual probing is
more purely functional and always serves worthy purposes. It
might be said, therefore, that his sight is more American (functional, clarifying) than European (romantic, mysterious).
Leatherstocking's vision helps to distinguish his heroism from
the derivative Byronism that characterizes the Pilot, and identifies him as Cooper's most fully American hero.

Because the poetic, contemplative vision of Deerslayer and
Emersonian transcendental seeing are both characterized by
an essential passivity, they would seem to be closely related
modes of appropriating the landscape. But there are crucial
differences between them. Poirier, in arguing the similarity of
the visual functions of Deerslayer and Emerson's poet, cites a
phrase from the opening passage of *The Pathfinder.* But a fuller
section of that passage shows how dissimilar these modes of
seeing really are:

> The sublimity connected with vastness is familiar to every
> eye. The most abstruse, the most far-reaching, perhaps

9. *The Poetics of Reverie*, pp. 184–85, 196.

the most chastened of the poet's thoughts, crowd on the
imagination as he gazes into the depths of the illimitable
void. The expanse of the ocean is seldom seen by the
novice with indifference; and the mind, even in the
obscurity of night, finds a parallel to that grandeur, which
seems inseparable from images that the senses cannot
compass. With feelings akin to this admiration and awe—
the offspring of sublimity—were the different characters
with which the action of this tale must open, gazing on the
scene before them. Four persons in all—two of each sex—
they had managed to ascend a pile of trees, that had been
uptorn by a tempest, to catch a view of the objects that
surrounded them. [1]

The first thing that can be said about Cooper's celebration of
vastness is that its tone is noticeably cooler than Emerson's
evocation of the powers of the transparent eyeball. It contains
none of the verbal extravagances that characterize Emerson's
attempt to force language to describe the motions of the soul.
There is none of the breathless phrasing, the dashes of thought
that work to communicate the simultaneity of the experience:
"I become a transparent eyeball. I am nothing. I see all. The
currents of the Universal Being circulate through me; I am
part or particle of God." Instead, Cooper uses a language
which John Lynen has correctly identified as "official." [10] Not
only in its formal and predictable rhythms but also in its use of
accepted terms of landscape description—"awe," "sublimity,"
"grandeur"—it offers an essentially *public* view of nature, not
the personal and subjective acount we find in Emerson.

Here there is no attempt to fuse the self momentarily with
nature through the act of perception; rather, all the terms of
Cooper's description suggest that the (appreciative) response
of *his* poet takes for granted a separation between the observer

10. Lynen writes, "By holding us within an official language, the style [of
Cooper's *The Pioneers*] makes our experience collective; by holding Natty at a
distance as an object in a setting, it makes his response to nature an aspect of
our response to landscape" (*The Design of the Present*, pp. 194–96).

and the landscape, affirming a relationship which can be defined as that of spectator and scene. As we have noted, Cooper felt no need to confront the problem of Lockean dualism; indeed, his aesthetics depend on such an understanding of the relationship between nature and the human mind.

While Emerson's moment of transcendence is necessarily private and subjective (although it has democratic implications), the celebration of natural beauty in the opening scene of *The Pathfinder* is not diminished by the presence of "Four persons in all." This is because the landscape they view is, perceptually, common property. All of the characters can, and ought to, respond to it in the same way—according to an objective code of moral and aesthetic value. For Cooper, the experience of viewing nature is, at its most rewarding, a matter of recognizing inherent and universal truths. Landscape is *available* for inspiration and moral lesson, not *usable* in the Emersonian sense of the highest (symbolic) use of nature. As Cooper indicates, the "sublimity" he describes is "familiar to every eye."

Transcendental writers like Thoreau and Whitman employ verbs such as "swimming" and "floating" to emphasize the fluid relationship between self and world as well as to suggest the transforming (artistic) power of the self, but these verbs are hardly to be found in Cooper's prose. Nature, for him, is not a mutable ambience which can serve the integrating eye; it is, rather, an objectively knowable constant which pleases and enlightens because of its permanent and inherent capacity to do so. Seeing provides a direct appropriation of "truths," but it is not a creative act of assimilation and transmutation.

Cooper's great impatience with moral shortcoming may be attributable, in part, to this understanding of the relationship between seeing and knowing. If all that is required is to look and learn, then moral laxity can only be regarded as obtuseness or, perhaps more accurately, blindness—a quite literal inability to *see*. Cooper's understanding of the function of sight, then, relates to his pessimistic view of human nature as essentially fixed, and ultimately to his sense of historical doom. The vision of the transparent eyeball, on the other hand, expresses Emerson's characteristic optimism by implying a belief in the human capacity for change and organic growth, possibilities open to everyone.

The moral dynamics of Cooper's fiction are created by setting figures who are insensitive to nature's lessons, like Harry March in *The Deerslayer*, against those, like Leatherstocking, who attend to them. In a broader sense, the natural world is the constant by which men can measure the progress or demise of their culture, for nature will remain when vast and powerful civilizations have come and gone.[11] It is the essence of Leatherstocking's identity that he is as constant, as timeless, as nature itself. In narrative terms, he is a "flat" character in the same way as Cooper's landscapes are immanent.[12] Not only is he continuous with nature, he is also an embodiment of the code that prescribes man's most elevated response to it.

When one knows and respects the code, then all one must do is assume the proper point of view. In the opening scene of *The Pathfinder*, the four characters scale a "pile of trees" in order to afford themselves the most advantageous view of their surroundings. The placement of these characters upon an elevated point serves to demonstrate that, in Cooper's fictional world, the emphasis is less on the self than on the world that selves inhabit. His fiction does not depend upon the development of a central perceiving eye, as does, for example, the work of Henry James—a writer who clearly was influenced by Emerson.

Emerson's perspectivalism, which makes the self-reliant spirit the absolute locus of perception, stands in contrast to Cooper's use and understanding of point of view. In Emerson,

11. Thomas Cole, the American painter whose work parallels Cooper's in many ways, dramatizes this theme in *The Course of Empire,* a series of paintings the novelist admired greatly. See *L&J*, 5:397–98.

12. See R. W. B. Lewis on Leatherstocking as "the hero in space" (*The American Adam,* pp. 98–105); Charles A. Brady on the hero of *The Spy* as "a mythopoeic emanation" of the landscape ("Myth-Maker and Christian Romancer," p. 72); Marius Bewley, *The Eccentric Design,* p. 73; Donald A. Ringe, *James Fenimore Cooper,* p. 28; and John Lynen, pp. 178–79, 189.

certain conditions of environment are better than others for transcendental experience, but the *point* of view is less important than the condition of the viewer. For Cooper, however, the selection (or discovery) of the appropriate perspective has greater importance. In one of his travel journals, he records the following observation: "Here one of the sweetest and most striking views I had seen in Switzerland met me unexpectedly. Took a position a little on one side and directly on the verge of a perpendicular rock that completely commanded the whole landscape. At our feet lay a perfectly level plain, at the distance of more than [a thousand] 500 feet, sprinkled with houses, and covered with the most delicate verdure" (*L&J*, 1: 316). The view is "sweet" and "striking" because of the particularly favorable circumstances of the moment. As we saw earlier, surprise always enhances landscape for Cooper, so the fact that the scene comes upon him in his way—"met me unexpectedly"—is essential to the experience. Equally favorable is the position of elevation on which the viewer finds himself. As in the scene from *The Pathfinder*, the distant view of nature gives the spectator complete "command," and the experience of embracing the whole makes the "far view" of the landscape the one that Cooper most valued.

In this description, the conditions of surprise and elevation are totally circumstantial; they owe nothing to the sensitivity or even to the anticipation of the viewer. But Cooper is not quite content with this happy accident, for he takes further "steps" to enhance the view. He tells us that he "took a position" in order to compose the scene (to make a "picture" of it). His intention, however, is not to transmute the visual into the visionary but merely to frame the landscape properly. He composes it not in the sense of creating but in the sense of ordering and arranging, or making calm and tranquil. These latter meanings communicate best Cooper's understanding of his artistic function as an observer, and as a writer. Although he would have agreed that to determine the most advantageous perspective is to perform an embellishment, he would have called this a modest function which does not alter one's basic perception of reality.

To take "a position" is merely a way of ascertaining the "true" image of the landscape, in much the same way that Cooper ascertained the truth of Jefferson's character in Thomas Sully's portrait.

In *The Deerslayer*, after Leatherstocking and Harry March see the Glimmerglass for the first time from the hills above, they descend to the shore and venture onto the surface of the lake in a canoe which "glided across the placid sheet." "Several times," Cooper writes, "the men ceased paddling, and looked about them at the scene, as new glimpses opened from behind points, enabling them to see further down the lake, or to get broader views of the wooded mountains." "The only changes, however," he continues, "were in the new forms of the hills, the varying curvature of the bays, and the wider reaches of the valley south" (35). The qualifying phrase, "only changes," indicates that although the viewers' perspective shifts as the canoe glides down the lake, no new angle of vision alters their sense of the whole. We have seen how, for Emerson, the gaining of "perspective" is a highly subjective experience which can give the perceiver "an original relation to the universe" (7). But in this passage the shifting perspective brings only a slightly modified, more detailed view which is validating rather than transforming. The essential meaning of the landscape is as clear and obvious at the first observation from the hilltop as at the second or third from the lake below. As John Lynen says, Cooper's objective is "to create the immediacy of direct perception by making it seem that the things viewed exist independently in themselves, quite unaffected by the personality of a particular observer" (197–98). But the landscape rendered here is unaffected by its observers in another sense too, for the phrase "only changes" also suggests the timelessness and absolute permanence of the scene, a scene which cannot be altered by man. As we shall see, Cooper's commitment to such permanence—philosophical, moral, and psychological—was large.

These observations express in another way what has long been recognized, that Cooper's ties to eighteenth-century

thought are very strong. While he is romantic in that he conceives of nature as the region of possibility and freedom, his
artistic sensibility derives from neoclassicism. As Patricia
Spacks has said, poetry as well as the other arts in the
eighteenth century were regarded as "essentially imitative,
offering a reflection of the real world."[13] One prominent aes-
thetician of the period, Hugh Blair, writes, "Description is the
great test of a Poet's imagination."[14] By using the word "description," neoclassical theorists meant to emphasize *accurate*
representation. It is not surprising, therefore, to find Cooper
objecting to a work of fiction because of its failure to present
accurate images. As I noted earlier, his response to Scott's
nautical tale, *The Pirate*, was that while it rendered a "vrai-
semblance" of life at sea, it did not depict that life accurately.
His answer to Scott was *The Pilot*, a novel he said would create
"truer pictures of the ocean and ships" (viii).

Standing behind the requirement for "truer pictures" is an
assumption concerning the way the eye works. Locke himself,
whose theory of perception underlies eighteenth-century
aesthetics, had made it clear that by vision he meant the literal
faculty of seeing, not a metaphoric extension of the power.[15]
Later, when nineteenth-century romantic poets were reacting
against Locke's thought, vision came to imply something
beyond the power to re-present. As a recent essay shows, vision
in Wordsworth's poetry provides anything but a direct perception of the world; it serves, instead, as "an almost diagrammati-
cally regular bridge between stages of consciousness, a con-
struction of mutually canceling connotations which makes the
movement from blankness to brilliance a progression by stages
rather than leaps."[16] Romantic poets in general expressed a
distrust of the literal faculty of seeing because it seemed to
them to intensify the problem of Lockean dualism—the sep-

13. *The Poetry of Vision*, p. 5.

14. *Lectures on Rhetoric and Belles Lettres*, 2:37 (cited in Spacks, p. 5.).

15. See Jean Hagstrum, *The Sister Arts*, pp. 137–38.

16. Kenneth R. Johnston, "The Idiom of Vision," in *New Perspectives on
Coleridge and Wordsworth*, p. 17.

aration of self from world. Because seeing is the most imper-
sonal and distant means of perception, dependence upon it
emphasized for them the space between themselves and nature. As Tony Tanner has written, "To be linked to a thing only
by sight is at the same time to be severed from it, if only because
the act of purely visual appropriation implies a definite space
between the eye and the object."[17]

But Cooper's favorite nature poets were James Thomson
and Thomas Gray,[18] not Wordsworth. And the work of these
writers illustrates what Jean Hagstrum calls the "widespread
acceptance in the eighteenth century of this Lockean idea
[Locke's insistence on the literal power of sight]," an idea which
"gave new importance to *ut pictura poesis*. Poetry, like painting,
is closely related to the art of actual seeing: the poet too must
have seen and must be able to cause others to see."[19] When we
consider that the two Romantics whose work probably
influenced Cooper the most—Byron and Scott—are themselves figures with strong links to eighteenth-century thought,
the difference between Cooper's vision and transcendental
vision becomes even more clear. As we have seen, then, we
must distinguish from Emersonian seeing both the analytical
visual powers of Cooper's heroes and the contemplative, ap-
preciatory sight of his "poets." For the novelist's landscapes
make their lessons—both practical and moral—known to us
directly.

An important paradox exists, however, in Cooper's and
eighteenth-century poets' response to nature. While they
claimed that their art brought *real* nature into view, the landscapes they produced were strongly influenced and informed
by earlier pictorial art. E. H. Gombrich, in *Art and Illusion*, says
that "nature could never have become 'picturesque' for us
unless we, too, had acquired the habit of seeing it in pictorial
terms" (266). Gombrich argues convincingly that all paintings

17. "Notes for a Comparison between American and European Romanticism," p. 89.
18. See Susan Fenimore Cooper's remarks in *Pages and Pictures*, p. 17.
19. *The Sister Arts*, p. 138.

"owe more to other paintings than they owe to direct observation" (268) and that "only a picture painted can account for a
picture seen in nature" (265), an argument which can be extended to literary representations of nature as well. Cooper's
concern for accurate description, then, is based on an illusion,
for "accuracy" is itself a pictorial convention, a schema associated with the neoclassical view of the world. It can be said of
Cooper, as Marshall McLuhan and Harley Parker say of the
eighteenth century, that he "was dedicated to the proposition
that the outer world existed to end in a picture."[20] The beginning passage of *The Wing-and-Wing* describes a portion of the
Mediterranean Sea as an "unrivalled sheet dotted with sails,
rigged, as it might be, expressly to produce effect in a picture"
(9). And in a travel book, *Gleanings in Europe: England*, Cooper
makes the following observation: " I have great pleasure, as the
season advances, in studying the varying aspects of the parks,
which, at moments, present singularly beautiful glimpses. The
chiaro scuro of these pictures is not remarkable, it is true; the
darks predominating rather too much." "This is a bold criticism," he adds, "considering that nature is the artist" (2:28). In
such descriptions, nature seems simply to present itself as a
painting, creating the illusion that the composing eye has done
none of the work. The assumption, of course, is closely related
to Cooper's (and the eighteenth century's) view that nature is
an orderly system. And from Natty Bumppo, who finds his
lessons in the woods, to Roswell Gardiner (of *The Sea Lions*),
who discovers order in the stars, Cooper's virtuous characters
use their sight to affirm that the universe possesses a comprehensible design.

Gombrich's work helps us clarify Cooper's understanding of
the meaning of visual experience. But to say that the writer's
"pictures" are reflections of the way his age saw nature does not
explain the appeal of his landscapes. If we were to apply
Gombrichian analysis to Cooper's work, we would cite all those

20. *Through the Vanishing Point*, p. 121.

conventions from earlier pictorial and literary forms that seem
to have influenced him. We would say, for example, that poets
such as Thomson taught him to conceive of nature in terms of
certain scenic effects and to see it as a "picture." The paintings
of the Hudson River School of artists, as well as their immediate predecessors, would have to be cited, but we would
also have to trace a European landscape tradition back at least
as far as Claude Lorrain and Nicholas Poussin. We know that
from Ann Radcliffe and Charles Brockden Brown, Cooper
learned to find in the natural world aspects of the gothic. Sir
Walter Scott clearly gave him the notion of landscape as a
"context," as a historical setting for romantic action. And we
would have to add that there is nothing particularly revolutionary about the strong visual emphasis of his work, that
Bryant's poetry and the fiction of Scott and Maria Edgeworth
are also highly pictorial. But having ascertained all of this, we
would still not know precisely why Cooper's work has power.[21]

Cooper's imagery is the subject of part II, but here I can
indicate the direction of our probe. Gombrich argues that all
ways of seeing the world are learned and cites the "apparent
vault of heaven" as a case of "the need for some initial assumption."[22] The heavenly vault is one of the images which has an
important place in Cooper's fictional world. It forms the out-
ermost circle in a series of architectonic enclosures consituted
"first [by] the branches of the trees, and then [by] the deep,
fathomless vault of heaven for a canopy" (*OO*, 351). In his
fiction, this image establishes for the reader a sense of "inti-

21. A perennial and perplexing question. Among the many who have asked
it are Norman Foerster, who cites Balzac's well-known amazement at the way
Cooper's landscape "passes into you, or you into it, and you know not how this
metamorphosis, the work of genius, has been accomplished," and then agrees
that the manner in which Cooper "achieves his effects is something of a
mystery" (*Nature in American Literature*, p. 5). With a different focus, R. W. B.
Lewis speculates upon "why it is always so hard to locate the source of Cooper's
power: we look for it in the wrong places and, not finding it there, are inclined
to deny its existence" (101).

22. *Art and Illusion*, p. 232. Also see pp. 214–15.

mate immensity,"[23] of a world vast and sublime but also enclosed. And I think we should ask if this is not an example of
what Gombrich, in *Meditations on a Hobby Horse*, calls a
"psychologically grounded minimum image" (8). In defining
this term Gombrich argues for the existence of very basic
schemata whose presence "is always felt" (8), schemata which
reflect a biological and psychological need to find in the world
certain valued configurations (the human face, for example).
Such an image is "psychologically grounded" in that it is unsophisticated (unlike a "conceptual image," which originates at
a higher level of schematization). And it is a "minimum image"
because it creates form out of the smallest amount of visual
data which "will make it fit into a psychological lock," a lock
closing at a "primitive level" (8) of perception. The existence of
such basic schemata, Gombrich believes, explains our feeling
that "there are certain privileged motifs in our world" (6).

Isn't it possible that the sky seen as an overarching dome is
such a privileged motif? Perhaps we see it in this way because of
our resistance to the idea of a spatially unlimited universe,
because of our need for a world "contained." To visualize the
sky or the uppermost level of the forest interior as a canopy is,
as Gombrich says, an illusion; but the image-making involved
in the creation of this illusion may originate at a deep level. As
we have seen, Cooper's naive response to the visual image is
basic in just this sense. Unlike the pictorialism of later (symbolist) writers, his work presents an essentially unsophisticated
treatment of space. And in our exploration of his fictional
landscapes, we shall be attentive to those privileged motifs that
evoke in us our most fundamental sense of being in the world.

23. This phrase is the title of chap. 8 of Bachelard's *Poetics of Space*.

PART II

The Lovely Openings

Mr. Cooper was much struck with a remark on the size of the forest-trees of America, smaller than was anticipated, scarcely equal in size, it was asserted, to those of the older parks, and churchyards and village greens of England. One is scarcely prepared indeed for this result of civilization; we should rather have believed that the pride of the forests would naturally reveal itself in grander forms within the bounds of the wilderness—that the fostering care of man could do little for the woods. Such was then, the usual American idea on this subject; but we are beginning, it is hoped, to learn another lesson, to discover that the forests and groves are one of the higher forms of husbandry.

Susan Fenimore Cooper, *Pages
and Pictures from the Writings
of James Fenimore Cooper*

3

The Reign Below: The Interiorization of Wilderness Space

> The American forest exhibits in the highest degree the grandeur of repose.
>
> *The Wept of Wish-ton-Wish*

For Cooper, the sea was the essential wilderness. It was the setting against which he measured all other forms of wilderness space, a savage, unpredictable antagonist which even the greatest of heroes looks on with dread. There is no doubt that the awesomeness of the sea thrilled Cooper, and he used "the wilderness of the ocean" (*RR*, 256) to provide the broadest possible field of action for his boldest heroes, all of whom have an insatiable appetite for adventure and require the " 'tempestuous ocean for a world' " (*WW*, 461). Their fiercest combatant is always the sea itself, and it is clear that Cooper's land heroes can manipulate their environment more successfully than can his nautical heroes. Natty Bumppo dies of old age on the prairie, but Tom Coffin (of *The Pilot*) perishes in a shipwreck.[1]

Cooper's nautical tales are interesting and important; as Thomas Philbrick has shown, they made possible the development of American sea fiction.[2] But despite Philbrick's ambitious attempt to claim for them a very high place in Cooper's canon, I do not think the modern reader finds these works as appealing as the forest novels. Leslie Fiedler suggests a reason: "If Cooper never managed to write a romance of the

---

1. See Philbrick, *James Fenimore Cooper and the Development of American Sea Fiction*, pp. 67–68.
2. See his book cited in note 1.

39

sea as satisfactory as his romances of the forest, it was because
he knew the sea too well, approached it not as a dreamer but as
an expert."[3] This remark is helpful because it articulates the
profound difference we sense between the worlds of Cooper's
nautical and forest fiction. And to emphasize this difference is
salutary because most critics have not done so. Rather, they
have misapplied the generalization made by R. W. B. Lewis in
The American Adam: "For Cooper the forest and the sea shared
the quality of boundlessness: they were the *apeiron*—the area of
possibility" (99). Lewis's virtual equation of the space of forest
and sea has validity and importance as long as it is held within a
historical (or "mythic") framework. But when this formula is
applied loosely to describe the pictorial qualities of Cooper's
work, it oversimplifies. Indeed, in most discussions of the writer's landscapes, the word "boundless" (or "vast") has been
used so sweepingly and indiscriminately as to have become a
cliché. As we shall see, Cooper's woods do communicate a sense
of boundlessness, but this is only one of their characteristics.

Fiedler's observation is helpful, then, but it puts too much
emphasis on the writer's approach to materials (dreamer versus expert) and on a matter of relative knowledge. There is a
sense in which Cooper dreamed the woods, but he also
dreamed the sea. And it isn't true that he knew the sea better,
only that he knew it differently, conceived it as a different kind
of space. The "illimitable waste of water," as Cooper sometimes
calls the ocean, is an immense world starkly constituted of two
elements, water and sky, which often appear as a single, infinite
ambience. The "open sea" is in constant flux, but paradoxically, it is also "vacant and without change" (*WW*, 459). Its uni-
formity of color and texture as well as its constant motion
make it a "trackless waste," a setting which necessitates a different kind of movement through space than is required by the
forest. As Leatherstocking observes in *The Pathfinder*, " 'Water
is the only thing in natur' that will thoroughly wash out a trail' "
(30). And we have seen how Cooper's nautical heroes must rely

3. *Love and Death in the American Novel*, p. 188.

almost exclusively upon the most abstract of the senses, the eye, and upon instruments which depend far more upon the sky than the earth.

It is true that some of Cooper's land novels are set in scenes of unmitigated visual immensity which strongly suggest the space of the ocean, and we are all familiar with the vast, barren landscape of *The Prairie*. We know that in writing this novel Cooper adopted the visual schema of his sea fiction (he had not seen the western plains at the time of composition), and the fact that *The Prairie* contains many more sea images than any of his other land novels[4] merely confirms the point. The following passage is representative: "The earth was not unlike the ocean, when its restless waters are heaving heavily, after the agitation and fury of the tempest have begun to lessen. There was the same waving and regular surface, the same absence of foreign objects, and the same boundless extent to the view" (14).

It is not important that in employing such a schema Cooper misrepresented the prairie and created something very close to a desert, except to point out that in his imagination the values of ocean and desert are almost identical. Both worlds are desolate and harsh, resistant to human imprint and habitation, and the men who traverse them are susceptible to all of nature's adverse forces. Like the ocean, the prairie is a masculine world associated with "wildness and adventure" (14) and one in which the sky, the traditional domain of male gods, is the dominant, even overwhelming, environment.

The "absence of foreign objects" and the "sameness of the surface" (15) enforce a view of barrenness and featurelessness that can be defined as *"visually undifferentiated waste."* This phrase, borrowed from Edward T. Hall's study of human spatial needs,[5] refers to landscapes which lack the visual clues by which men usually make their way in the world. In *The Prairie*, Cooper depicts a landscape almost devoid of the verti-

4. Philbrick, *James Fenimore Cooper and the Development of American Sea Fiction*, p. 297n.

5. *The Hidden Dimension*, p. 80.

cal structures that give form and texture to his forest settings
and make pathfinding artistic rather than arduous. There is
even reason to believe that he conceived the prairie as a kind of
anti-forest, for in this novel Natty tells Ishmael Bush, " 'I often
think the Lord has placed this barren belt of prairie behind the
States, to warn men to what their folly may yet bring the land' "
(27). Later, he insists in a discussion with Doctor Bat that the
Garden of Eden could only have existed in the space of the
forest: " 'the garden of the Lord was the forest then, and is the
forest now, where the fruits do grow and the birds do sing,
according to his own wise ordering' " (246).[6] Unlike the textured and fruitful space of the woods, the prairie is a barren
world[7] which is experienced horizontally; its space reaches far
into the lateral distance without interruption where, like the
sea, its "waves" blend into the infinite ambience of the sky.

In one of Cooper's sea novels, *The Water Witch*, the variety
and fruitfulness of land space are compared with the "vacancy"
of the ocean, as one of the characters is invited to " 'go deeper
into the country, and see more of its beauties—its rivers, and its
mountains—its caverns and its woods. Here all is change, while
the water is ever the same' " (459). Although this particular
character (a cabin boy) chooses the sea as his "home" (the plot
and spirit of the book demand it), I think Cooper might have
agreed with Claude Lévi-Strauss, who muses in *Tristes
Tropiques*: "It seems to me that the sea destroys the normal
variety of the earth. Enormous spaces and supplementary
colours it may offer to the eye—but at the price of a deadening
monotony, a flat sameness, where never a hidden valley keeps
in reserve the surprises on which my imagination feeds" (332).

It is this variety (and security) that moves Miles Wallingford
to ecstasy when he returns from a harrowing sea voyage to the

6. See Ringe, *The Pictorial Mode*, pp. 50–51. Also see Leatherstocking's fear
of "prairies" in *The Pathfinder:* " 'I have heard . . . that the finger of God has
been laid so heavily on them, that they are altogether without trees' " (103).

7. Also see Cooper's rendering of the "sublime sterility" (227) of the Sahara
in *Homeward Bound* and the "sterility, and chill grandeur" (265) of Antarctica in
The Sea Lions.

beautiful Hudson River Valley in *Afloat and Ashore* (the title identifies the polarity): "Clawbonny never looked more beautiful than when I first cast eyes on it that afternoon. There lay the house in the secure retirement of its smiling vale, the orchards just beginning to lose their blossoms, the broad rich meadows, with the grass waving in the south wind, resembling velvet" (115–16). Although the pastoral estate of Clawbonny does not lie within the space of the wilderness, Cooper's woods are characterized by the order and plenitude of this setting. By contrast, the ocean is devoid of such pastoral imagery.

In the scene from *The Pathfinder* that we examined in the previous chapter, four characters ascend a thirty-foot pile of trees on a hilltop in order to witness the distant view of nature. Seen from the level of the treetops, the forest does look like the ocean, an "ocean of leaves" (3). The "waves" of foliage extend into the distance in a solid mass, until they terminate at the horizon, "blending with the clouds" (3). From this elevated perspective, Cooper allows his characters to witness "the vastness of the view, the nearly unbroken surface of verdure, that contained the principle of grandeur" (3). As has often been noted, *The Pathfinder* is a particularly aqueous land novel, containing many sea images. What has not been properly emphasized is the principle of selection at work in the employment of these images. Nautical metaphor inevitably comes into play when the narrator or the characters assume the "far view" of nature, the elevated view that affords the widest angle of vision. It is significant that while sea imagery gets heavy use in Cooper's land novels, the analogy does not tend to work the other way.[8] The only two land metaphors that appear with any frequency in his descriptions of the sea are "prairie" and "desert," and these exceptions confirm the spatial identity of Cooper's ocean and prairie.

Cooper's woods share with his ocean and prairie the aspect

8. Thomas Philbrick says this "process consisted in part of the translation of the unfamiliar into the familiar" (*James Fenimore Cooper and the Development of American Sea Fiction,* p. 297n).

of immensity. But where the latter two settings sustain a single vision of vastness, his novels of the forest merge the immense with the intimate, creating a blend of spatial values. Cooper's forest is at once dangerous and protective, open and enclosed, limitless and delimited, difficult and amenable, wild and formal. One might discuss this merging of values in terms of the eighteenth-century landscape norms of the beautiful, the picturesque, and the sublime,[9] and these terms will find application in this analysis. But they are a part of the vocabulary of Cooper's time, not of ours; what we require is a language flexible enough to describe the felt design of the writer's spatial world, not one that even at the time of its inception was regarded by many as an oversimplified and arbitrary categorization of human responses to nature.

That Cooper's woods are rendered as a mixture of contrasting spatial values is evident in the following passage of description from one of his forest novels, *The Wept of Wish-ton-Wish*: "the vaulted arches beneath are filled with thousands of high, unbroken columns, which sustain one vast and trembling canopy of leaves. A pleasing gloom and an imposing silence have their interminable *reign below,* while *an outer and another atmosphere* seems to rest on the cloud of foliage" (423; my italics). The interrelation between these two realms, the "reign below" and the "outer atmosphere," is of crucial importance in any discussion of the aesthetics of Cooper's forest novels.

When the four characters in *The Pathfinder* descend from the observation point referred to earlier, we find them in a "windrow," a variety of clearing which Cooper describes in this way: "a sort of oases [*sic*] in the solemn obscurity of the virgin forests of America" (1). The interior realm of the forest that exists beneath the "vaulted arches" and "canopy of leaves" is arranged by Cooper into a network of valued enclosures: "covers," caves, huts, and clearings. Where the space of the "outer atmosphere" is visually undifferentiated, the space of the in-

9. Others have done so. For example, see Alan F. Sandy's unpublished doctoral dissertation, "The Sublime, the Beautiful, and the Picturesque in the Natural Description of James Fenimore Cooper."

terior forest is highly structured, and the clearing, with its
carefully drawn perimeter, is the archetypal space of the "reign
below."

Cooper's use of the word "oases" suggests more than the
shape of the clearing; it brings to mind the amenity we associate with such space. (Natural clearings, of course, are to be
distinguished from those created by the axe. In Cooper's
novels, the latter are often associated with wanton destruction.)
In his study of the aesthetics of nature, Paul Shepard writes that
the clearing is experienced as an inverse oasis, "an island of
open space in the continuum of forest." Shepard reminds us
that, in old Saxon, paradise was translated as meadow.[10]

Although the clearing, or glade, has been treated as idyllic
space in Western literature from the earliest times, the
eighteenth century made a special response. In an evocatively
titled essay, "The Room Outdoors," Geoffrey Grigson describes how the eighteenth-century English imagination was
prepared by the paintings of Claude Lorrain and the poetry
of John Milton to give intense value to the natural glade (or
"lawn," as it was called). The clearing had come to be closely
associated with pastoralism and innocence, and was also regarded as one of the most certain indices of the order God had
established in the natural world. An exciting "confirmation" of
nature's order came in 1740 with the discovery of Tinian in the
Marianas, an island covered with lovely natural clearings. According to an early account by Richard Walter (cited by Grigson), the woods in Tinian "were in many places open, and free
from all bushes and underwood, so that they terminated on the
lawns with a well-defined out-line . . . but the neatness of the
adjacent turf was frequently extended to a considerable distance, under the hollow shade formed by the trees." "Hence
arose," Walter continues, "a number of the most elegant and
entertaining prospects, according to the different blendings of
these woods and lawns" (26). As Grigson points out, such
descriptions inspired the creation of the "Tinian lawn" in English landscape gardening.

The "hollow shade formed by the trees" was appealing to the

10. *Man in the Landscape*, p. 77.

eighteenth-century imagination (and to our own) because of its appearance of domestication; in reality a natural landscape, Tinian seemed to have been prepared especially for habitation by man, creating the effect of a "room outdoors." Here we should recall that in this same period neoclassical aestheticians such as Addison were arguing that while nature is superior to art, it is most appealing when it most closely resembles art. As Addison wrote in his *Spectator* papers treating "The Pleasures of the Imagination" (1712), "But tho' there are several of those wild Scenes, that are more delightful than any artificial Shows; yet we find the works of Nature still more pleasant, the more they resemble those of Art" (66). And Leo Marx has shown us in *The Machine in the Garden* that Addison's reconciliation of garden and forest "points toward the pastoral image of America" (93). James Fenimore Cooper is an inheritor of these aesthetics, and we can find in his woods many clearings which evoke the same quality of amenity as does Walter's description of Tinian.

But here it is necessary to make a distinction between the rhetoric of Cooper's fiction and the force of his imagery. For while many of his novels render the pervasive amenity of the forest, his work has often been linked with that of earlier writers who had visualized the woods as a region of difficulty and terror. Although Cooper stands outside the Puritan tradition that finds expression in Hawthorne's works as a profound fear and distrust of nature, there is no doubt that he felt the impact of early American conceptions of the wilderness as obstacle. A more direct influence, however, is the gothic fiction of Ann Radcliffe and Charles Brockden Brown. It is true that Cooper was affected by the work of these writers,[11] but his use of the language of gothicism is often not wholly convincing, and we are left with a discrepancy between rhetoric and image. The difficulty can be resolved, I think, by examining Cooper's narrative technique, for while the writer often *refers* to the wilderness as harsh and terrifying, he seldom actually de-

11. See Fiedler, pp. 196–97; Sandy, pp. 87–115.

scribes this aspect of the woods.[12] For contrast, let us examine a
passage from Brockden Brown's *Edgar Huntly*:

> No fancy can conceive a scene more wild . . . than that
> which presented itself. The soil was nearly covered with
> sharp fragments of stone. Between these, sprung bram-
> bles and creeping vines, whose twigs, crossing and in-
> tertwining with each other, added to the roughness below,
> made the passage infinitely toilsome. Scattered over this
> space were single cedars with their ragged spines and
> wreaths of moss, and copses of dwarf oaks, which were
> only new emblems of sterility. . . . In a wilderness like this
> my only hope was to light upon obscure paths made by
> cattle. Meanwhile I endeavoured to adhere to one line,
> and to burst through the vexatious obstacles which en-
> cumbered our way. The ground was concealed by the
> bushes, and we were perplexed and fatigued by a continual
> succession of hollows and prominences. At one moment
> we were nearly thrown headlong into a pit. At another we
> struck our feet against the angles of stones. The branches
> of the oak rebounded in our faces or entangled in our
> legs, and the unseen thorns inflicted on us a thousand
> wounds. . . . Sometimes we lighted upon tracks which
> afforded us an easier footing and inspired us with courage
> to proceed. These, for a time, terminated at a brook or in a
> bog, and we were once more compelled to go forward at
> random. [174–75]

In all of Cooper's fiction, there is not a scene comparable to
this, either in its intense particularity or in its subjection of the
characters to the tortures of the underbrush.[13] His narrator
frequently tells us of the "impenetrable" quality of the wilderness but seldom shows us a character negotiating such terrain.

12. Obvious exceptions are *The Last of the Mohicans* and certain of Cooper's
other early works. See my discussion of "the landscape of difficulty" in part 3.

13. As Edward Everett Hale, Jr., points out, the intense particularity of this
passage makes it somewhat unusual even for Brown ("American Scenery in
Cooper's Novels," p. 327).

By holding the "impassable" aspect of the woods at a narrative distance, Cooper is able to convert it into an object of aesthetic interest, treating it as picturesque or sublime. Typically, we find his characters just emerging from the kind of space that Brown, in the passage cited above, chooses to describe in detail. The beginning passages of both *The Pathfinder* and *The Deerslayer* show the characters moving from the density of the forest into the preferred space of the clearing. In *The Deerslayer*, Cooper makes us aware that it has been necessary for Natty Bumppo and Harry March to labor through thick underbrush to reach the Glimmerglass, but our first actual contact with these figures comes in this way:

> At length a shout proclaimed success, and presently a man of gigantic mould broke out of the tangled labyrinth of a small swamp, emerging into an opening that appeared to have been formed partly by the ravages of the wind, and partly by those of fire. This little area, which afforded a good view of the sky, although it was pretty well filled with dead trees, lay on the side of one of the high hills, or low mountains, into which nearly the whole surface of the adjacent country was broken.
>
> "Here is room to breathe in!" exclaimed the liberated forester, as soon as he found himself under a clear sky, shaking his huge frame like a mastiff that has just escaped from a snow-bank; "Hurrah! Deerslayer; here is daylight, at last, and yonder is the lake." [15–16]

A few pages later, after Hurry Harry and Deerslayer have reconnoitered this clearing, they proceed toward the Glimmerglass, only a short distance away, and Cooper comments upon their new surroundings: "The forest was dark, as a matter of course, but it was no longer obstructed by underbrush, and the footing was firm and dry" (29). At the point that the real action of the novel begins, the region of "impassability" is behind them, and they now inhabit the "pleasing gloom" that is the characteristic space of the interior forest. As Cooper writes in *The Wept of Wish-ton-Wish*, the "lower scene" possesses "a freshness which equals that of the subterranean vault, without possessing any of its chilling dampness" (423). The *described* space of Cooper's forest novels has much more in common with Walter's rendering of Tinian than it does with the tangled and pitted woods of Brockden Brown.

There are indications that throughout his life Cooper hoped to find his own American Tinian, an ideal natural landscape, and he seems to have found it in the woods of western Michigan on a trip in 1847, an experience which prompted him to write *The Oak Openings*. If *The Prairie* stands at one pole of Cooper's imaginative geography, then this late novel stands at the other. The two titles themselves supply us with the basic spatial tension that exists throughout his work: vastness and sublimity versus enclosure and amenity.

All of Cooper's tales of the woods evoke the amenity of enclosed space, but *The Oak Openings* offers a sustained view of the forest interior. Criticism has generally treated (and dismissed) this novel as an example of the intense religious and social conservatism that finds expression in Cooper's late works,[14] yet it can as fruitfully be seen as a celebration of discovery, a discovery of an edenic landscape which answered the writer's deepest sense of what nature *ought* to look like.[15] He begins the novel by observing that the "American forest has so often been

14. For example, see Kay S. House, *Cooper's Americans*, pp. 249–60; George Dekker, *James Fenimore Cooper the Novelist*, pp. 246–47; John P. McWilliams, Jr., *Political Justice in a Republic*, pp. 291–97. In my analysis, I will deliberately ignore those matters of ideology and religious conviction (the episodes relating to the conversion of Scalping Peter, for example) focused upon by other critics. But it should be noted that although Cooper is dealing in this novel with materials of landscape which might have resulted in one of his finest works, the pervasive didacticism of the book nearly ruins its effects. I use it here to illustrate the specific means by which Cooper pastoralizes wilderness space and do not intend to give it new importance in Cooper's canon, except on these terms.

15. Cooper's surprise at the stunning beauty of the oak openings was genuine. As James Beard writes, he had come to Michigan not as a sightseer or as "a novelist gathering materials for a book" (*L&J*, 5:219) but for land negotiations. Alan Sandy notes that the landscape of *The Oak Openings*, like that of *The Deerslayer*, conforms to the eighteenth-century aesthetic category of the Beautiful (p. 14).

described, as to cause one to hesitate about reviving scenes that
might possibly pall, and in retouching pictures that have been
so frequently painted as to be familiar to every mind" (10). But,
he urges, if the reader will "bury himself with us, once more, in
the virgin forests of this widespread land," he will "discover
new subjects of admiration" (10). For Cooper, the new subject
of admiration was the oak forest of western Michigan, a region
he describes as "the garden of America" (29). The novel's hero,
Ben Boden, theorizes that that " 'most beautiful garden' " in
which God placed Adam and Eve was " 'some such place as
these openings, I reckon' " (246).

Paul Shepard has written that the garden, "midway between
nature and art," is "the perfect human habitat": "It is designed
to provide the best of all possible relationships to nature, un-
impaired by the practical routines of house and field. It combines fruitfulness, refuge, and the deepest insights into the
living world" (117). *The Oak Openings* satisfies every aspect of
this definition. It has the most consistently drawn edenic landscape in all of Cooper's fiction, and the identity of the hero is in
full consonance with the setting. Ben Boden is characterized as
a "man of gentle and peaceable disposition . . . [who] had ever
avoided those scenes of disorder and bloodshed, which are of
so frequent occurrence in the forest and on the prairies" (64).
He is a bee-hunter, and, as Henry Nash Smith has pointed out
in a different context, this profession frees him "from even the
justifiable taint of bloodshed involved in Leatherstocking's vocation."[16] Cooper makes it clear that bee-hunting is to be distinguished from other forms of the hunt: "Of all the pursuits
that are more or less dependent on the chances of the hunt and
the field, that of the bee-hunter is of the most quiet and placid
enjoyment." "He has," Cooper adds, "the stirring motives of
uncertainty and doubt, without the disturbing qualities of bustle and fatigue; and, while his exercise is sufficient for health,
and for the pleasures of the open air, it is seldom of a nature to
weary or unnerve." Ben practices his vocation with an ease of

16. *Virgin Land,* p. 76.

intuition and a "gentle excitement" (66) that identify him
closely with the pastoral setting he inhabits.

Throughout the novel, Cooper's imagery works to domesti-
cate and pastoralize the space of the oak openings. Like the
island of Tinian, this landscape is admirable because it so
closely resembles art: "The region was, in one sense, wild,
though it offered a picture that was not without some of the
strongest and most pleasing features of civilization" (10). The
oaks in some places "stand with a regularity resembling that
of an orchard" (11) and in others are "scattered profusely over
the view, and with much of that air of negligence that one is apt
to see in grounds, where art is made to assume the character of
nature" (10). But the most lovely scenes are to be found among
the "spaces . . . of singular beauty, [which] have obtained the
name of 'openings' " (10). These interludes of "grassy glades"
within the continuum of forest "bear no small affinity to artificial lawns" (11) and resonate of the amenable space of a "room
outdoors." They establish the design of the classical clearing in
Cooper's fiction and appropriately give this novel its title.

But the action of the novel extends beyond the area of "the
lovely openings" (307) to the space of more open prairie land,
and the difference between Cooper's treatment of that terrain
in this novel and in *The Prairie* is striking. Instead of a vast,
sublime landscape without boundary, here he depicts a pastoral, flower-covered expanse whose name, "Prairie Round,"
suggests its definition: "This well-known area is of no great
extent, possessing a surface about equal to that of one of the
larger parks of Europe" (308). Like the openings, Prairie
Round (which Cooper informs us derives from the French
phrase for "round meadow") bears the "stamp of seeming
civilization—seeming, since it was nature, after all, that had
mainly drawn the picture" (307).

As these passages demonstrate, almost the entire geography
of *The Oak Openings* is pastoralized, a fact which makes the
novel unusual. Cooper is careful to point out that "the 'openings' had not the character of ordinary forests. The air circu-
lates freely beneath their oaks, the sun penetrates in a

thousand places, and the grass grows, wild but verdant. There was little of the dampness of the virgin woods" (42–43). None of Cooper's other forest tales as thoroughly domesticates the wilderness. We need only think of *The Last of the Mohicans* to realize that elsewhere in his fiction, the writer's landscapes are less consistently edenic. Yet even a novel like *The Last of the Mohicans* contains "islands" of pastoral space described in the same terms as "the lovely openings." *The Oak Openings*, therefore, makes possible an intense examination of the valued spaces that appear more intermittently but just as evocatively in all of Cooper's forest fiction.

In a later chapter I shall consider more fully the "dialectics of outside and inside"[17] that create the spatial tension of Cooper's novels. Here I am principally concerned with examining the images that constitute the "inside." But in order to make such an examination, it is necessary to suggest the general nature of this opposition. The archetypal space of the "inside" is the clearing, and Cooper's narratives would not develop at all were it not for the arenas of human action that they provide. But the clearing itself would have no status or even existence without the "outside," the vast, surrounding forest that forms its boundary. "Inside" and "outside" are utterly dependent on one another for meaning and establish their value by contrast. Where the forest is "infinite," "trackless," and disorienting (creating the danger—and excitement—of being lost), the clearing offers enclosure and a sense of location. When Natty Bumppo and Harry March break into the clearing described earlier, they suddenly know where they are. And where the forest is "impenetrable" and full of difficulty and danger, the clearing offers refuge.

In fact, all of the open spaces in Cooper's forest can be thought of as varieties of the clearing, for all partake of the essence of interiority. Even Prairie Round is described as a very large glade, bounded on all sides by the woods. Some clearings

17. The phrase is Gaston Bachelard's. It is the title of chap. 9 of *The Poetics of Space*.

are fully contained by a canopy of leaves overhead; others
stand like temples with an opening to the skies. The classic
underforest of Cooper's fiction is like a clearing because of its
dry and carpetlike surface and because of its openness. The
trees grow "to a great height without throwing out a branch,"
making it possible for the eye to "penetrate to considerable
distances." Hardly a thick and tangled maze of growth, the
underforest is depicted as highly structured space, constructed
by a series of "high and gloomy vaults" and a "dome of leaves"
(*D*, 303, 121). Lakes function in a similar way. Natty Bumppo
unmistakably regards the Glimmerglass as a form of clearing
and finds "a pleasure in studying this large, and, to him, unusual opening into the mysteries and forms of the woods" (*D*,
45). For him, the lake is a larger version of the "wind-row,"
answering the needs of those who " 'have bigger longings in
that way' " (285).

   In the following two chapters, with *The Oak Openings* as our
point of reference, we shall examine a series of images and
structures—first those which formalize and humanize the
space of Cooper's woods, and then those which impart to them
the qualities of amenity and enclosure. But as we make this
examination, we must keep in mind a distinction between the
writer's use of individual metaphors and the overall effect of
his imagery. Such a distinction is especially important in the
study of a novelist like Cooper, whose metaphors sometimes
seem stereotyped and worn but whose overall effect is power-
ful. Our ultimate concern is the way in which these contigu-
ous images interlock to form a complete structure, and we are
seeking to discover what Bachelard calls the preferred image,
the image that gives unity to a writer's world.

4

Finishing the Landscape

The walk, for a mile, was along an excellent carriage road,
and through meadows of exquisite delicacy and verdure,
among fruit trees and all the other accompaniments of
rural beauty. I can cite to you nothing with which to
compare the neatness and velvet-like softness of the
fields, but those of dooryards in our prettiest villages; for,
in the way of agriculture on a great scale, we have nothing
that is comparable.

Sketches of Switzerland, part 1, vol. 1

Much has been made of Cooper's remarks in his contribution
to *The Home Book of the Picturesque*, where he declares that
European scenery "offers to the senses sublimer views and
certainly grander, than are to be found within our borders,
unless we resort to the Rocky Mountains, and the ranges in
California and New Mexico" (52). But not enough attention
has been given to another observation from the same essay:
"The great distinction between American and European scenery, as a whole, is to be found in the greater want of finish in
the former than in the latter" (52). As important as the deficien-
cies of American mountains when compared to the Alps was
America's lack of "finish." Cooper's travel books and journals
are filled with admiring references to the "neatness" of European landscapes and rural scenes. His commentary on a small
Dutch village is typical: "[Our guide] took us round the Town,
and showed us all the Wonders—the greatest wonder however
is the air of neatness, and order, that prevails throughout."[1]

1. *L&J*, 1:265. In one of his travel books, Cooper writes, "One hears a great
deal of the magnificent mountains of Switzerland, while too little is said of the
rare beauty of its pastoral lowlands" (*Sketches of Switzerland*, pt. 1, 1: 56).

The polar terms scattered throughout the journals are "regular" and "neat," "irregular" and "broken," and Cooper's preference for the former mode is unmistakable. Occasionally, he comes upon a scene which reminds him of home: "The country very broken and irregular. Valley narrow but no high mountains visible. For many miles the country now strongly resembled the newest and most [wild?] parts of America" (*L&J*, 1: 335).

When we consider that for Cooper, the American wilderness appeared "broken and irregular," it becomes easier to understand his celebration, in *The Oak Openings*, of the beautifully arranged topography of the oak forest of western Michigan. Cooper goes on in *The Home Book of the Picturesque* to argue that in America "the accessories are necessarily wanting, for a union of art and nature can alone render scenery perfect" (56). And in one of his travel books, he refers to "that pleasing mixture of nature and art that is wanting in America, but which abounds over all the more ancient regions of the eastern hemisphere."[2] We have seen how the pervasive imagery of *The Oak Openings* is that of park and garden, images which suggest the presence of art and "embellish native scenery" (308). The narrator of another late novel, *The Redskins*, is a man who, like Cooper, has spent several years abroad before returning to his American home. His comparison of European and American scenes reflects Cooper's own responses:

> But it is certain that, as a nation, we have yet to acquire nearly all that belongs to the art I have mentioned that lies beyond avenues of trees, with an occasional tuft of shrubbery. The abundance of the latter, that forms the wilderness of sweets, the *masses* of flowers that spot the surface of Europe, the beauty of curved lines, and the whole finesse of surprises, reliefs, backgrounds and vistas, are things so little known among us as to be almost "arisdogratic," as my Uncle Ro would call the word. [184]

With its landscape composed of "many a glade and . . . many a

2. *Sketches of Switzerland*, pt. 1, 1:29.

charming grove" (68), *The Oak Openings* is the most thoroughly Europeanized of all of Cooper's novels about the American wilderness. The "park-like 'openings' " (68) possess all the "accessories" that give nature its finish, and the fact that these are natural accessories makes the setting all the more interesting: "There were the glades, vistas, irregular lawns, and woods, shaped with the pleasing outlines of the free hand of nature, as if consummate art had been endeavoring to imitate our great mistress in one of her most graceful moods" (309).

When the narrator of *The Redskins* speaks of "the beauty of curved lines," he is referring to the variety he found characteristic of European landscapes. But Cooper's use of the "curved line" also lends itself to formality, and *The Oak Openings* is one of the writer's most formal settings. Although he is careful to avoid an absolute symmetry in his arrangement of elements, he draws a landscape that is, if anything, more formal than the space of a European park. The openings are rendered as gently described circles of meadowland, and Prairie Round, which has all the attributes of "a well-kept park" (307), has "so near an approach to a circle as to justify the use of the appellation" (308). Cooper deliberately introduces irregularities into this landscape to add elements of contrast and other aspects of the picturesque, but these touches do not disguise his basic impulse toward an intense formality.

Prairie Round is formalized not only by its circular shape but also by the arrangement of elements within its perimeter. An "island of wood" (314) rests at its exact center, establishing a focal point which organizes the inner space of the circle. And this "island-like copse" (319) contains at *its* center a secret clearing bounded by a "belt of hazles" (324). A valued center-point surrounded by one or a series of concentric circles is one of Cooper's most characteristic structures. We can find it in any number of his other works, but perhaps the most familiar example is *The Deerslayer*, where Muskrat Castle lies near the center of the Glimmerglass, with a "belt" of forest surrounding on every side. To gain this degree of centrality, Cooper had to give up a certain amount of geographical verisimilitude, but the fact that he made the change (explained in his preface to the novel) is instructive: "The shoal on which Hutter is represented as having built his 'castle' is a little misplaced, lying, in fact, nearer to the northern end of the lake, as well as to the eastern shore, than is stated in this book" (xiii).

The circle is unquestionably the basic figure in Cooper's fictional design; its circumference separates the clearing within from the wilderness beyond, and this dialectic of inside and outside embraces a whole range of contrasting values. But the circle also functions as the clearest expression of Cooper's desire to formalize the space of the American woods with "the beauty of curved lines" and, as we shall see presently, to heighten the theatrical effect of the forest scene.

The term *scenery* comes from the Greek word for stage, a derivation suggestive of Cooper's treatment of landscape. The early nineteenth-century novel was heavily influenced by the theater, and especially by its melodramatic effects, but Cooper was more interested in the drama's formality and scenic quality than in its emotional intensity. It is widely recognized that, as one critic puts it, he "tended to frame his novelistic action in dramatic terms—setting a scene, moving his characters into it, building to a confrontation, resolving the action, closing the scene."[3] Usually this pattern is discussed in relation to its effect on characterization and plot, but just as important is its effect on the setting itself. For a writer who conceives of his setting as a stage will inevitably create a fictional world different from that of writers who draw narrative space in more novelistic terms.

Cooper's books are organized into highly formalized scenes which are as distinctly separated from one another as scenes in a stage play are individualized into units by the closing and opening of the curtain. The characters are often held for an entire chapter within a setting so tightly framed that it reminds us of the proscenium arch of a stage, and when Cooper

3. John Seelye, "Some Green Thoughts on a Green Theme," p. 604.

changes the scene, he does so in an extremely deliberate fashion: "We shift the scene. The reader will transfer himself from
the valley of the Wish-ton-Wish to the bosom of a deep and
dark wood" (*W*, 422). The effect of holding characters within a
carefully delimited scene is similar to the pictorial quality of
history paintings, such as Benjamin West's *The Death of Wolfe*
(1770). In that work, the distant background is filled with
action and turmoil, but the foreground holds the principal
figures in a timeless moment.

  Cooper's fiction tends to move forward, not progressively or
fluidly but haltingly, from one such individuated moment to
another. This scenic quality is heightened by the narrator's
tendency to dwell on landscape description, so that large blocks
of novelistic "space" are consumed in a minimal amount of real
time, creating a condition of profound narrative stasis.[4] Ian
Watt's generalization that the novel as a form distinguished
itself from the classical theater by creating a more human,
realistic sense of the passage of time[5] is only partly true of
Cooper's work. Again, a discrepancy forms between rhetoric
and image. On the one hand, he is a realistic novelist, attending
carefully to matters of chronology; but the overall spatial and
temporal effect of his fiction is extremely classical and static.

  The Oak Openings provides a perfect example of the theatrical
quality of Cooper's work, for the glades that structure the
space of the novel serve as theaters in the round, separate and
well-defined centers of human action and deliberation. The
characters are introduced in the following manner: "The sun
was already approaching the western limits of a wooded view,
when the actors in its opening scene must appear on a stage
that is worthy of a more particular description" (10). While the
stage metaphor is commonplace in the fiction of Cooper's time,
it has special significance in his work, especially as it conjoins

  4. Gerard Genette defines narrative stasis as a category of fictional duration
in which "the narrative discourse continues while historical time is at a
standstill, usually in order to take care of a description" ("Time and Narrative
in *A la recherche du temps perdu*," in *Aspects of Narrative*, pp. 101–02).
  5. *The Rise of the Novel*, pp. 21–25.

with the other images that tend to frame and formalize his narrative space.

All of the human action in *The Oak Openings* is stagelike, but the most densely theatrical scenes are those Cooper invests with ritual and ceremony. At a crucial point in the development of the narrative, the chiefs of the various Indian tribes gather at night in the forest to decide the fate of Ben and his white companions. They meet in an area "so formed and surrounded as to have something of the appearance of the arena of a large amphitheatre" (255). Typically,Cooper places two "spectators," Ben and Corporal Flint, in a hiding place on the edge of the clearing to provide a visual and psychological perspective for the reader. From this hidden spot, the two observers witness a "picture [which] might be described as imposing to a degree that is seldom seen in the assemblies of the civilized" (260). With a fire burning in the "precise center" (255) of this natural arena, the chiefs sit in a circle which conforms to the larger circle formed by the clearing's edge, thereby intensifying the quality of centralized and concentrated space. Even before the Indians have begun their deliberations, Cooper has created a scene thickened and charged by the flickering light of the fire and by the anticipation of ritual, a scene he describes with a strange mixture of gothic and pastoral images: "Nothing could have been more unearthly than the picture presented in that little, wood-circled arena, of velvet-like grass and rural beauty" (256).

The scene is reminiscent of many of the famous Indian ceremonies in Cooper's fiction, such as those which take place in the Mingo and Delaware camps in *The Last of the Mohicans*. But it has most in common with the Huron encampment in *The Deerslayer*. The natural setting for this camp is almost identical to one of the oak openings; with its "resemblance to a densely wooded lawn" and its "appearance of sward" (505), it is one of Cooper's classical forest clearings. The writer's use of the clearing in this case shows how he was able to exploit such encircled space for heightened dramatic effects.

Cooper prepares us for the climactic torture scene of *The*

Deerslayer by first giving us a nighttime view of the camp. Assuming much the same perspective of amazement and awe as taken by Ben Boden and Corporal Flint, Deerslayer and Chingachgook spy upon the Hurons from the top of a nearby ridge. Through their eyes we witness the same mysterious fire and ghostly shadows—a scene, says Cooper, that "Salvatore Rosa would have delighted to draw" (300).

It is during the torture scene that follows the next day that the Huron camp assumes its most formal and theaterlike character. The forest serves as the outer wall of the setting while the Indian braves form an inner circle with the bound Deerslayer at its center. This scene is dominated by the Indians in more than a literal sense, for the space within the inner circle has become electrified with the rhythms of primitive ritual and the wall of warriors prevents any violation of its integrity.

As the torture begins, several of the novel's principal actors successively have their moments on this elaborately prepared stage, each in an attempt to save Deerslayer. First Hetty "appeared in the circle" (547), but neither her entrance nor Judith's subsequent "admission" to the "circle" (554) disturbs the intensity of the ceremony. Next, Cooper tells us that Hist "pushed through the circle" (564) into the arena, but as before, the cordon effectively seals itself. It is Chingachgook's bounding into "the very center of the circle" (567) which finally causes it to rupture, because his entrance signals the arrival of the white soldiers from the fort. Quickly the torture ends and the stage itself is dismantled. Its actors are dispersed and many of them are killed.

This pattern of spatial concentration and dispersion will concern us directly in part III, but here it should be pointed out that in Cooper's fiction white men, especially military forces, interrupt and disrupt the primitive unity of the Indian world. The circle represents the cohesion and concentration of ritualized space, while the straight lines of military formation intersect and break apart the "curved lines" of the natural world. In this scene the soldiers advance with a "regular and heavy" (568) tread, unmindful of the natural formations of

[handwritten annotations at top: "remember in settlements / setting — church + fort / contradiction"]

nature. The resulting conflict has none of the formal beauty of Indian combat; instead, "wild confusion, despair, and phrensied efforts were so blended as to destroy the unity and distinctness of the action" (569).

As we shall see in the discussion that follows, those who use nature best in Cooper's world follow their vocations and found their settlements in accordance with the already established designs of the natural world. Of all these characters, the Indian is the most sensitive to these designs, as demonstrated by his appropriation of the natural clearing for his habitation and the performance of ritual. In the scenes described above, the space of the clearing is put to its most dense and theatrical use; to its pastoral definition is added the charge of high drama.

It may surprise us to find Cooper employing the image of a settlement to enhance the value of the wilderness, yet this is what he does in *The Oak Openings*. Prairie Round not only resembles a large European park but also suggests to him "the site of some old and long-established settlement from which every appliance of human industry had been suddenly and simultaneously abstracted." "Of houses, out-buildings, fences, stacks, and husbandry," Cooper explains, "there were no signs; unless the even and verdant sward, that was spread like a carpet, sprinkled with flowers, could have been deemed a sign of the last" (308–09).

In our readings of Cooper, we may have been too much influenced by the rhetoric of Natty Bumppo, a figure whose role commits him to a systematic verbal attack on settlements. And it is possible that the very high place among Cooper's works that criticism has given to *The Pioneers* has caused us to overemphasize or perhaps misinterpret the issue of civilization *versus* nature in his fiction. The greatness of *The Pioneers* is its sensitive and detailed rendering of a frontier community. It effectively dramatizes the destructive forces of the settlement stage of civilization with the pigeon-shoot, the fish-kill, Billy Kirby's wood chopping, Hiram Doolittle's careless architecture, a reckless mining expedition, and a forest fire. Its atten-

tion to the details of life in Templeton makes it one of the
writer's most realistic novels.[6] But we tend to forget that this
kind of realism is not characteristic of Cooper. Although he
often theorizes in his other works about the settlement stage,
nowhere else does he focus so closely upon the day-to-day life
of a frontier community.

Cooper more characteristically describes a distant and more
beautiful past, as he does in novels like *The Water Witch* and *The
Deerslayer*, or he advances through time to a period during
which established estates are being threatened by social and
political forces, as he does in *Home as Found* and *The Redskins*.
But even in works in which he treats the settlement stage of
development, he generally finds ways to minimize those aspects of frontier life focused upon in *The Pioneers*.

A good example of this technique is *Wyandotté*, a novel in
which an explorer in prerevolutionary times discovers a beautiful lake in the wilds of New York State. Captain Willoughby
removes the beaver dam that created the lake and thereby exposes an expanse of rich soil which becomes the site of a settlement. Although he experiences guilt over his destruction of
the lake, it is explained that this act has enabled him to avoid all
those "unsightly" features that usually accompany the development of civilization: "All this . . . had Captain Willoughby escaped, in consequence of limiting his clearing, in a
great measure, to that which had been made by the beavers, and
from which time and natural decay had, long before his arrival,
removed every ungainly object . . . giving to these places the
same air of agricultural finish" (62–63). Here we do not find an
antagonistic relationship between the settlement and nature;
rather, a beautiful agrarian community that has grown up
almost overnight exists in a state of perfect harmony with the

6. Thomas Philbrick has correctly pointed out that, contrary to traditional
readings of *The Pioneers*, this novel is hardly an idyllic treatment of a frontier
community. At best, Philbrick argues, it is a case of ironic pastoral, for Cooper
continually draws our attention to ugly contention, disorienting change, and
efforts to harm the natural world ("Cooper's *The Pioneers*," pp. 588–90). Also
see Donald Ringe, *James Fenimore Cooper*, pp. 32–37, and my discussion in
chap. 6, pp. 102–07.

surrounding wilderness: "The site of the ancient pond was a miracle of rustic beauty. Everything like inequality or imperfection had disappeared, the whole presenting a broad and picturesquely shaped basin, with outlines fashioned principally by nature, an artist that rarely fails in effect" (63).[7]

Wyandotté is only one of several Cooper novels in which a favorable natural setting makes possible an aesthetic union of wilderness and agrarian images. In *The Wept of Wish-ton-Wish*, the narrator describes a lovely Connecticut valley which holds a small Puritan settlement existing in "strong and pleasing contrast to the endless and nearly untenanted woods by which it was environed" (30). The initial scenes of *The Red Rover* are set in the "enticing and lovely" colony of Rhode Island. This prerevolutionary " 'Garden of America,' " whose "neat and comfortable villas, lay sheltered in groves, and embedded in flowers" (15), is surrounded by the "wilderness of the ocean" (256) and by the "endless and unexplored wilderness" (17) of America. And in *The Chainbearer*, the settlement of Ravensnest has quickly taken on the appearance of "an old country" (128), because of its location and circumstances. It stands in a pocket of pastoral space, "garnished with broad meadows" and "enriched by fields" (128), with a "background . . . [of] the 'boundless woods' " (129).

These examples show that the agrarian image was a highly positive one for Cooper,[8] especially when juxtaposed in "pleasing contrast" with the unbounded wilderness. In most of his novels about this stage of civilization, he found ways to mitigate the deforming visual effects of the settlement, effects which had captured his attention in *The Pioneers*. In this respect,

7. See Susan Fenimore Cooper's account of her father's attempt to avoid the destructiveness and unsightliness of the settlement stage in his development of a family farm in the woods near Cooperstown (*Pages and Pictures*, pp. 347–48).

8. Among the "pictures" that Cooper's European visitor, in *Notions of the Americans*, finds most pleasing are those of the New England countryside. Deeply impressed by the "space, freshness, [and] an air of neatness and of comfort" of the villages, he also celebrates the pastoral scenes of cattle "grazing in the fields" and flocks "clipping the closer herbage of the hill sides" (1: 60–61).

Cooper is like Thomas Cole and William Cullen Bryant who, as Charles Sanford has observed, "tried to merge the two images of rural earth and sublime nature into a single image." [9]

Thus it should not surprise us to find Cooper embellishing the natural scenery of the oak forest with images of husbandry, especially when those images depict "an old and long-established settlement." Used in this way, they create the illusion of a history; they mellow the space of the wilderness and suggest the possibilities of art and human control. When Cooper describes the openings as "lovely rural scenes," he reveals his wish to see the wilderness as *settled* space.

Although all the glades in *The Oak Openings* possess beauty and amenity, the one that contains Ben Boden's hut has special significance: "The 'chienté,' or shanty of le Bourdon [Ben Boden] stood quite near to the banks of the Kalamazoo, and in a most beautiful grove of the burr-oak. Ben had selected the site with much taste, though the proximity of a spring of delicious water had probably its full share in influencing his decision" (28).

This beautiful clearing is the center of the narrative in several important ways. First, it serves as the established point of return; the action begins here, moves to a point further down the Kalamazoo, and then returns for the climactic scenes of the novel. This is the fixed point that organizes and makes comprehensible all the rest of the novel's geography. But it has further significance as a center. The "spring of delicious water," the great beauty, amenity, and protection afforded by the glade—all these give it strong edenic associations. [10] Because it is bordered by a "beautiful sward" and is garnished with an "abundance of flowers," we are not surprised that Ben should have "selected it for his principal place of residence" (430).

9. *The Quest for Paradise*, p. 142. See Leo Marx's well-known discussion of "the middle landscape" (pp. 220–26, passim). For an example of this merging in the visual arts, see George Caleb Bingham's painting, *Missouri Landscape*.

10. The word *paradise* derives from the Old Persian word for enclosed park or orchard.

person (moral power) proceeding from a source

But while the existing natural attributes of this setting influenced Ben to choose it as his home, the fact of his choice gives added value to the site. The accepted equation in critical discussions of the relationship between character and setting in Cooper's fiction is that figures like Natty Bumppo are "emanations" of the wilderness, that they take their definition from nature and would have no identity without it. But the reverse is also true. The presence of characters like Natty and Ben Boden helps to define and enhance the natural world. Ben has chosen to found a world in this place, and his act of appropriation intensifies its human value.

It might be argued that Natty Bumppo programmatically avoids founding a world in this sense. And it is true that after *The Pioneers*, the first-written of the Leatherstocking tales, Natty has no regular abode; instead, the forest becomes his home. But within the expanse of wilderness, certain key sites take on special meaning because they are identified with his past in the woods. In *The Last of the Mohicans* the waterfall hideout and the deserted blockhouse in the forest are rich with the association of previous expeditions. The site that gains most from such association is Lake Otsego, the setting of *The Deerslayer, The Pioneers,* and *Home as Found.* At the end of *The Deerslayer*, Natty and Chingachgook return to the Glimmerglass fifteen years after the events of the novel. Because of historical accident, this "gem of the forest" has not been visited by man in all those fifteen years and remains a scene of "magnificent solitude," "a spot sacred to nature." But it is sacred in another sense too, for the setting continues to bear the imprint of these two warriors' "First War-Path." Deerslayer and Chingachgook nostalgically investigate the "picturesque ruin" (595–96) of Hutter's castle and examine the other remnants of their adventure. To make the association even more resonant, Cooper looks ahead in this passage to the burial of Indian John (an event which takes place in *The Pioneers*) in these same hills many years later. And long after Leatherstocking's time, one of the characters in *Home as Found* refers reverentially to a " 'spot hallowed by a deed of Natty Bumppo's' " (145).

Cooper's novels play significantly upon such associations; part of the pleasure of reading them is our recognition of places we have imaginatively visited before. In this way, Cooper lays out a historical geography of the nation, a geography which compensates for the ruined castles America lacked. This suggests the writer's distinctive role as a historical novelist, for although he used many of Scott's techniques he did not so much refashion ancient legend in modern (romantic) terms as he created a "history" of America. As D. H. Lawrence said, Cooper invented America's youth.[11] And the youth he invented is inextricably identified with a single legendary character.[12] As we trace and retrace Leatherstocking's adventures through the wilderness, the places he touches are invested with meaning.

11. *Studies in Classic American Literature,* p. 54. Discussing *Home as Found,* Cooper tells his purpose in establishing a common setting for *The Pioneers* and the later work: "I had attempted to pourtray [*sic*] a peculiar state of society in its commencement [in *The Pioneers*], and by preserving this connection [in *Home as Found*], it saved much preliminary explanation, and enabled me to give a picture of the same again half a century later, and of obtaining some reflected interest for my scenes; a point of some moment in a country almost without a history" (*L&J*, 4:238). Cf. Thomas Cole, "Essay on American Scenery," pp. 11–12.

12. Recent criticism has tended to modify Arvid Shulenberger's contention that Natty Bumppo is the "major unifying element in the Leather-Stocking Tales" (*Cooper's Theory of Fiction,* p. 75); yet despite the very different functions Cooper has for Natty in the various tales, it seems to me that in our experience of reading, Leatherstocking's image has continuity.

5

The Forest Enclosure: Treasures
and Secrets

> Our house, apprehended in its dream potentiality, be-
> comes a nest in the world, and we shall live there in
> complete confidence if, in our dreams, we really partici-
> pate in the sense of security of our first home.
>
> Gaston Bachelard, *The Poetics of Space*

Ben Boden takes possession of his glade in the oak openings by
building a shanty which he affectionately calls "Castle Meal."
The name is actually "a corruption of *'Château au Miel'* " (30),
but in either the pure or corrupt form it suggests sustenance
and amenity. The shanty's utter simplicity and its organic
relationship to the environment link it to all the other legendary huts in Cooper's fiction. In *The Pioneers*, Natty Bumppo
inhabits "a rough cabin of logs, built against the foot of a rock"
(259), and Harvey Birch's secret hut in *The Spy* is also built into
the earth: "Three sides of this singular edifice . . . were composed of logs laid alternately on each other, to a little more than
the height of a man; and the fourth was formed by the rock
against which it leaned" (404).

Bachelard has written of the image of the hut, that its "truth
must derive from the intensity of its essence, which is the
essence of the verb 'to inhabit.' The hut immediately becomes
centralized solitude, for in the land of legend, there exists no
adjoining hut." Castle Meal is possessed of this legendary quality. It exists in a "remote . . . part of the world" (32), and
Cooper leaves no doubt that "Ben loved the solitude of his
situation" (34). His situation is analogous to the "deep forest
seclusion" (224) of Andries Coejemans in *The Chainbearer*. The

Chainbearer's hut, like Ben's, partakes of what Bachelard calls "the felicity of intense poverty," poverty which "gives us access to absolute refuge." [1] Cooper explains that it is "buried in the woods . . . , removed from the comfort, succor and outward communications of civilized life" (224).

Even larger and more elaborate structures in Cooper's fiction become imbued with the hut dream when they exist in a state of "deep forest seclusion." The subtitle of *Wyandotté* is *The Hutted Knoll*, a phrase which communicates well the integral relation between Cooper's huts and the earth. Although Captain Willoughby's building soon grows to a size and multiplicity of function that distinguish it from the simpler dwellings of Natty Bumppo and Ben Boden, its location deep in the wilderness preserves for it the name, "the hut," which it carries throughout the novel. Similarly, Thomas Hutter's castle in *The Deerslayer* maintains the amenity of primitivism because it is the "solitary [manmade] object" in the vast forest. While Hutter himself is a potential despoiler of nature, his castle (which is also referred to repeatedly as "the hut") is "in singular harmony with all the rest of the scene" (135).

Cooper's huts answer the needs of solitude, but they also provide protection against adverse forces. Ben's shanty "had been constructed with some attention to security" to protect him and his stores of honey from the two traditional enemies of a bee-hunter, "men and bears" (28). To "protect the honey," he takes the "unusual precaution" of barring his door with "three bars of oak," an act which "rendered all secure" (30). The fact that Cooper's fictional huts contain "treasures" like Ben's stores of honey gives further value to the space of their interiors, but it also makes them vulnerable to attack. This doubleness generates the basic tension of *The Deerslayer*, for Hutter's castle is identified both as a place of refuge and also as an enclosure which others desire to violate. The action of the entire novel is organized by a series of expeditions from and returns to this structure. Its white characters repeatedly flee toward "the centre of the lake" and the protection of enclosed

1. *The Poetics of Space*, p. 32.

space. But as the center, the castle also becomes the target, and the Hurons ultimately break into its interior. Anticipation of the moment of violation creates the novel's suspense, and in many of Cooper's works, this moment climaxes the action. This is true of *The Oak Openings*, in which the narrative tension builds toward the Indians' destruction of Ben's shanty.

As important as the treasures that huts protect are the secrets they contain. Natty Bumppo wages a continuing battle (in *The Pioneers*) to prevent the prying eyes of Templeton from discovering the presence of Major Effingham in his cabin, and Harvey Birch's hut holds the secret of Harper's real identity (George Washington). In *The Deerslayer*, a mysterious chest found in the castle is unlocked to expose not only such treasures as the chess pieces used in bargaining with the Hurons but also letters which bare the secret of Thomas Hutter's real identity and past transgressions. In each case, the reader's discovery of the nature of the secret resolves a conflict between appearance and reality and reveals past events which have an important relationship to the present. Cooper's huts, therefore, can be said to contain the secrets of the novels themselves, the answers to the ideological and moral questions they ask. The discovery of Major Effingham's presence, for example, clarifies the issue of the true ownership of the land.

But the chest in *The Deerslayer* contains other treasures which seem to have little functional importance: a dress, gloves, lace, a pair of pistols, and a navigational instrument. If we penetrate the surface of Cooper's official language, the scene in which Judith, Natty, and Chingachgook examine these items resembles nothing so much as children at play (they play in the absence of the novel's "adults," Thomas Hutter and Harry March). Yet this part of the narrative is far from unimportant. Judith's discovery of "a beautiful dress of brocade" brings this reaction: "Her rapture was almost childish; nor would she allow the inquiry to proceed until she had attired her person in a robe so unsuited to her habits and her abode" (227–28). The scene thus begins not with the probing of moral questions but with a game of "dress-up," a game of make-believe.

Although the chess pieces fashioned in the shape of animals

are used later in bargaining with the Hurons, they are initially perceived as wondrous playthings: "Even Judith expressed wonder as these novel objects were placed before her eyes." It is Chingachgook, however, who is most lost in "admiration and delight," particularly as he inspects "the elephants [which] gave him the greatest pleasure" (239). Similarly, the "admiration and surprise" expressed by Deerslayer and Chingachgook "at the appearance of the unknown [navigational] instrument, which was bright and glittering" (238), has about it the quality of childhood delight.

These "treasures" are not functional to the plot in the same way as the letters, but they are obviously more than mere decoration. For they are charged with the mystery that children impart to "magic" objects, and Cooper's treatment of them (and the characters) in this scene suggests one of the deep sources of his power. The discovery of treasure, the concealment and probing of secrets, the motions of hiding and emerging from cover—all of these are paradigms of children's games and products of a profound childhood imagination.

Especially paradigmatic is the response of Leatherstocking to the "pair of pistols, curiously inlaid with silver" (234). Chingachgook regards one of these ancient weapons as a " 'Child gun' " and handles it "as if it had been a toy." Deerslayer corrects his friend, saying, " 'Not it, Sarpent; not it' " (235), but then proves him right. Unable to resist the impulse to fire one of these pistols, he playfully engages his Indian friend in a competition and, as sometimes happens to curious children, the unfamiliar object explodes in his hand. The scene suggests the modern notion of children's play as experimentation toward mastery, the activity Erik Erikson calls the ego's "attempt to synchronize the bodily and the social processes with the self" and to practice these functions "in an intermediate reality between phantasy and actuality."[2] When we consider the extraordinary degree to which Leatherstocking's identity is defined by his ability to "do" (marksmanship, pathfinding, instructed seeing), then we can begin to understand how he

2. *Childhood and Society*, pp. 211, 212. Cf. Cooper's description of a "pair of curiously and richly mounted horseman's pistols" (405) in *The Spy*.

functions for Cooper as a representative of childhood—a stage of life in which psychic energy is focused upon skill acquisition and, as we shall see, upon a special (forest) environment ideal for "play."

As sensitive a reader of Cooper as D. H. Lawrence was, his division of the writer's personality into two opposing states of mind—*"Wish Fulfillment"* and *"Actuality"*—is misleading. Lawrence saw Cooper as a writer of split sensibilities, one side yearning for freedom and the woods and the other begging for recognition from the civilized (European) world. In architectural terms, he put "THE WIGWAM" against "MY HOTEL" as the polar structures of the author's imagination, suggesting that Cooper secretly dreamed of inhabiting a primitive forest dwelling while actually living a life of domesticated refinement.[3]

Lawrence's formulation sounds very much like Van Wyck Brooks's characterization, in *The Ordeal of Mark Twain*, of Twain as a writer whose talent was compromised by his needs for success and respectability. But Brooks on Twain is more convincing than Lawrence on Cooper in this respect, and nothing so clearly distinguishes the pastoralism of these two writers as their depictions of the space of human architectural structures. In Twain's classic work, *Adventures of Huckleberry Finn*, there are two prominent hutlike buildings, Pap's cabin on the Illinois shore and the shed on the Phelps farm where Jim is held captive. The first is the scene of Huck's confinement and near murder at the hands of his alcoholic father, and the second becomes a torture chamber for Jim. If huts in Twain's fiction are places of terror and imprisonment, houses are not much more habitable. Typically they are dominated by totalitarian women who subject boys to all the confining horrors of "sivilization." By contrast, nature is the place to which one escapes, the area of freedom and beauty, exemplified by life on a raft.

The pastoral of a book like *Adventures of Huckleberry Finn* might be called a pastoral of flight. It is defined almost exclusively by continual movements "away from," away from the

3. *Studies in Classic American Literature,* p. 48.

corruption and violence encountered at every point along the
Mississippi shore. If the necessity for flight disappears and the
characters cease to be in motion, as occurs in the last section of
the novel, the pastoral collapses. The "Territory" to which
Huck says he will flee has no convincing status in the imaginative life of the book, and the novel's conclusion suggests that
the writer has been unable to locate his pastoral.

Cooper's pastoral, on the other hand, is defined by stasis. His
work exhibits not the impulse toward flight but the desire to
arrive at a still point of the imagination, a place from which he
will never have to leave. It is the difference between escape and
retreat, a difference perfectly symbolized by the two representative structures of primitivism in the works of Twain and
Cooper: the raft (motion) and the hut (stasis). As we have seen,
Cooper's huts are centers of refuge and solitude, spaces to be
defended rather than escaped. And they are never in conflict
with nature but are in many ways continuous with it.[4] Civilization and nature are separate worlds for Cooper, but his imagery works to form an aesthetic union of the two. At its best,
civilization possesses the perfection of nature's design, and
nature at its loveliest has the appearance of high civilization.

Although Cooper's huts are located in remote parts of the
wilderness, and their hermitlike inhabitants such as Ben
Boden display a "passion for dwelling alone" (34), these primitive structures sometimes become houses and, ultimately, centers of civilization. When the narrator of *The Oak Openings*
returns to western Michigan many years after the events of the
novel, he finds the wilderness transformed into a scene of
agrarian beauty. The earlier images of husbandry can now be
understood as anticipatory; they represent the possibility, or
potential, of rural plenitude, which has now become a reality.[5]

4. Perhaps this explains why Leo Marx found a prominent place for Twain
in *The Machine in the Garden,* but almost none for Cooper, since the tensions
exhibited in Cooper's work are different from those Marx emphasizes in his
study of American pastoralism.

5. As John P. McWilliams, Jr., points out, the "fertility, beauty, and growth
of the oak openings have confirmed the [agrarian] dream" of America that
Cooper had posited in *Notions of the Americans.* As McWilliams implies, *Notions* is

Similarly, Captain Willoughby's primi.
grows into a large fortified structure at the
agrarian settlement. In *Satanstoe*, both the N.
the crude dwellings at Ravensnest are drawn
for fully developed centers of civilization. Ti
continuous with both nature and civilization, and
links the two worlds. (In *Home as Found*, the Effi
their family mansion "the Wigwam.") Cooper is or.
writers who, as Bachelard says of a French poet,   .nore
fortunate than dreamers of distant escape, in that he finds the
root of the hut dream in the house itself."[6]

But Cooper's vision of nature hardly requires such a linkage,
because his woods are themselves consistently imaged as a
house. In his forest novels, architectural metaphors often
dominate the descriptive passages.[7] Cooper saw the forest
variously as a temple, a church, a mansion—but whatever the
specific metaphor, the pervasive effect is that of a spacious,
highly structured interior. Here again is an image which informs both ways; the forest is beautiful because it resembles a
gothic cathedral, but as the narrator tells us in *The Deerslayer*,
"It was probably from a similar [natural] scene that the mind of
man first got its idea of the effects of Gothic tracery and
churchly hues" (508).

As I indicated earlier, the classic underforest of Cooper's
fiction is not a confusing maze of growth but is instead "free
from underbrush" and constructed of large, roomlike "vaults"
of space. The trees resemble "tall, straight, rustic columns" and
support a "dome" or "canopy" of leaves overhead. "Arches of
verdure" and "leafy entrances" provide the doors and hallways
that lead from one "room" to another. And within these vaults,
nature contains many lovely "furnishings": a "drapery of
forest," a "fringe of pines," a "broad carpet," a "bed" or

Cooper's political version of pastoral, and is to be contrasted with the "fault-
finding" of the *The American Democrat* (*Political Justice in a Republic*, pp. 295–96,
197).

6. *The Poetics of Space*, p. 31.

7. Use of the architectural metaphor in natural description is common in
Cooper's time. The most often cited example is Bryant's poem, "A Forest
Hymn."

lounge" of leaves. In *Satanstoe*, the narrator-hero describes a "hall":

> The ground fell away, in a sort of swell, for some distance in our front; and the trees being all of the largest size, and totally without underbrush, the place had somewhat of the appearance of a vast forest edifice, to which the canopy of leaves above formed the roof, and the stems of oaks, lindens, beeches and maples, might be supposed to be the columns that upheld it. Within this wide, gloomy, yet not unpleasant hall, a sombre light prevailed, like that which is cast through the casements of an edifice of the ancient style of architecture, rendering every thing mellow and grave. [424][8]

Natty Bumppo moves through the forest like a man walking through a very large, old, and familiar house, and he knows it as well. In *The Pathfinder*, he explains to Mabel Dunham how he " 'once made an appointment with the Big Sarpent, to meet at twelve o'clock at noon near the foot of a certain pine, at the end of six months, when neither of us was within three hundred miles of the spot.' " That they both found the tree at the appointed hour confirms the truth of Natty's declaration: " 'These are our streets and houses; our churches and palaces' " (290). In light of this, Leatherstocking's often cited remark from the same novel should be taken in a more literal (architectural) sense than it has previously: " 'I'm in church now; I eat in church, drink in church, sleep in church. The 'arth is the temple of the Lord' " (477).

Interiority is, of course, a feminine quality, and Cooper's houses and forest both radiate an intense feminine presence. The labyrinthine St. Ruth's Abbey of *The Pilot* is an environment "hermetically sealed against the world and its chilling cares" (105). And this setting of "peculiar comfort" (117) is closely associated with the novel's three female characters, who inhabit the ancient structure that once served as "the dor-

8. As Corny Littlepage discovers, this majestic "hall" contains the corpses of several of his companions. For the juxtaposition of natural beauty and danger in Cooper's fiction, see chap. 11.

mitories of the sisterhood" (116). Similarly, the gorgeous interior of the villa, Lust-in-Rust, in *The Water Witch*, is identified with its beautiful inhabitant, Alida de Barbérie.[9]

But even a relatively primitive dwelling can carry feminine value in Cooper's work. In *Satanstoe*, after Corny Littlepage and his party fight through the Indian enemy's lines to reach the safety of Ravensnest, the hero describes the sheltering, protective quality of this crude settlement-dwelling:

> It would not be easy for a pen as unskilful as mine, to portray the change from the gloom of the ravine, the short, but bloody assault, the shouts, the rush, and the retreat of the outer world, to the scene of domestic security we found within the Nest, embellished, as was the last, by woman's loveliness and graces, and in many respects by woman's elegance. [441]

The presence of a woman, Anneke Mordaunt, charges this interior with special value for Corny, and the motion he describes—from an "outer world" into a "Nest"[10]—indicates the basic "direction" of Cooper's pastoralism.

When the hero of *Lionel Lincoln* returns to America many years after his early childhood in Boston, he begins to remember the scenes of his youth. One of his most valued memories is of an old house he had inhabited as a child, and he recalls fondly "the days of my boyhood, and of my former freedom within its walls" (40).[11] The phrase, "freedom within its walls," perfectly characterizes the interiority of house and forest for Cooper. The house was not an entrapment or a

9. Ships, too, are feminine in Cooper's novels. See Philbrick, *James Fenimore Cooper and the Development of American Sea Fiction*, pp. 75–77. Also see Cooper's response to the splendor of Versailles in *Gleanings in Europe: France*, pp. 176–89.

10. See Bachelard on the phenomenology of nests, in *The Poetics of Space*, pp. 90–104.

11. The house of Cooper's own boyhood, and undoubtedly the model for many of his fictional houses, was Otsego Hall, a luxurious mansion which existed in harmony with the wilderness surrounding Cooperstown. For Cooper's description of the hall (constructed between 1797 and 1799), see *The Legends and Traditions of a Northern Country*, pp. 223–31.

prison but was instead a spacious and amenable enclosure whose counterpart was the "room outdoors."

We do not find in Cooper the intense ambiguity about home characteristic of many American writers. When he returned from Europe in 1833, he settled in the family mansion in Cooperstown, and his letters reveal the excitement of this return to "the scenes of my youth" (*L&J*, 3: 12). One of his first acts upon resuming residence in Cooperstown was to refurbish and partly reconstruct the badly deteriorated Otsego Hall,[12] an act which may have been symbolic of a desire to "reconstruct" and repossess the world of his childhood. That world was not one bifurcated into civilization and nature but a harmonious blend of what William Cullen Bryant identified as two of the primary elements in Cooper's childhood landscape: "the first house in Cooperstown" and "the vast forest around him."[13] These were complementary, not antagonistic, realms, and both were in need of defense.

Cooper's life and work reveal a high degree of anxiety over the violation of his personal space, and that space contained the woods as well as the house. Like the human structures in his fiction, his imagined forest also contains "treasures" and "secrets"; the Glimmerglass in *The Deerslayer* is "a gem of the forest" (595) which could be stolen by men like Thomas Hutter. The world of nature, "with its hidden, glassy lakes, [and] its dark, rolling streams" (114), that Cooper celebrates in *The Pathfinder* is a world in danger of attack and pillage. And like all those threatened and assailed dwellings in his fiction, the woods too could be destroyed by those who went about "laying bare the secrets of nature" (97) with the axe, as he warns in *The Chainbearer*. Although the plot of *The Pioneers* does not directly relate the burning of Natty Bumppo's cabin to the forest fire that ravages the woods around Templeton, these events are inti-

12. In a letter to Micah Sterling, dated October 27, 1834, Cooper described his plans for "repairing the Hall" and included a hand-drawn sketch of the building (*L&J*, 3:56).

13. In a eulogy delivered at Metropolitan Hall, New York City, on February 25, 1852. It has been reprinted widely, including its use as an introduction to the 1861 (Darley-Townscend) edition of *Precaution*; see pp. vi–vii.

mately related by the image of destruction by fire. In each case, uncontrollable greed is responsible. For Cooper, woodchoppers posed as clear a personal threat as the townspeople who tried to "steal" Three-Mile Point from his family.[14] Therefore, it is not contradictory, as some have judged it to be, for him to have defended the sanctity of the woods as vigorously as he defended the claims of personal property. This was not a case of conflicting democratic and aristocratic impulses but an expression of the fact that the perimeter of Cooper's personal space contained both the house and the woods as continuous elements in a valued landscape.

The setting of the marriage of Ben Boden and Margery Waring in *The Oak Openings* fuses the architectural metaphor with other key images to produce the most idyllic scene in the novel:

> A better altar could not have been selected in all that vast region. It was one of nature's own erecting; and le Bourdon and his pretty bride placed themselves before it, with feelings suited to the solemnity of the occasion. The good missionary stood within the shade of a burr oak, in the centre of those park-like Openings, every object looking fresh, and smiling, and beautiful. The sward was green, and short as that of a well-tended lawn; the flowers were, like the bride herself, soft, modest, and sweet; while charming rural vistas stretched through the trees, much as if art had been summoned in aid of the great mistress who had designed the landscape. When the parties knelt in prayer—which all present did, not excepting the worthy corporal—it was on the verdant ground, with first the branches of the trees, and then the deep, fathomless vault of heaven for a canopy. In this manner was the marriage benediction pronounced on the bee-hunter and Margery Waring, in the venerable Oak Openings. No gothic struc-

14. This famous dispute, in which the residents of Cooperstown claimed their right to use picnic grounds belonging to the Cooper family, is recorded in Cooper's letters; see *L&J*, 3:271–353. The events are dramatized in undisguised form in *Home as Found*.

ture, with its fretted aisles and clustered columns, could
have been one half as appropriate for the union of such a
couple. [350–51]

The marriage is important, because it suggests a conversion
of the dream of "forest seclusion" into the dream of Eden.
Early in the novel, Ben can be seen to cherish his solitude:
"Woman, as yet, had never exercised her witchery over him,
and every day was his passion for dwelling alone, and for
enjoying the strange, but certainly most alluring, pleasures of
the woods, increasing and gaining strength in his bosom" (34).
That was before he had met Margery, whose charms, in the
emotional logic of Cooper's novels, must replace the "pleasures
of the woods." As Ben explains it, before Margery arrived he
had not known " 'how much a woman can do in a *chienté*,' " but
now, " 'Woman has taken possession of my cabin.' " At first, it
appears that Cooper will for once allow the idyll of solitude to
be converted directly into Eden. Ben expresses his fondest
wish in the following passage: " 'I will come with you, Margery,
into these Openings, and we can live *together* here, surely, as
well, or far better than I can live here *alone*' " (344). But in
Cooper's novels, Eden is never to be,[15] for woman and the
woods exist in what might be called a substitutional or sublima-
tional relationship. Ben and Margery are forced out of their
paradise by hostile Indians who have been aroused by the
incendiary influences of the War of 1812. When the couple
eventually returns to the oak openings, they do so not as Adam
and Eve but as landowners. Ben sees action in the war and,
tested by experience, he becomes a prosperous gentleman
farmer, a figure of public importance. Cooper describes the
change approvingly, for it represents the necessary end of
innocence and the becoming of a man.

Ben's unrealized vision of a happy man and woman living
together in a cabin in the woods is, finally, an impossible

15. *The Crater* is an apparent exception. But although Cooper uses edenic
imagery to describe the life of Mark and Brigette Woolston, the setting is not
edenic in the sense described here. For by the time Brigette joins Mark on
Crater Island, the process of civilization building has already begun. See my
discussion of *The Crater* in chap. 9.

dream. Nowhere in Cooper's fiction is this impossibility stated more firmly than in *The Pathfinder*. More than a century of commentary and Cooper himself have identified this book as the Leatherstocking tale in which the hero falls in love (*L&J*, 4: 112). This *is* the central meaning of the novel, but its full significance is better understood within the context of the edenic dream than it is in terms of the romantic conventions of Cooper's time.

The final result is different, but Natty experiences the same transformation in *The Pathfinder* as Ben Boden does in *The Oak Openings*. The wilderness idyll is replaced in his consciousness by the love idyll, and he tells Mabel Dunham how former sources of reverie no longer satisfy him: " 'Before we met I had a sort of pleasure in following up the hounds, in fancy, as it might be.' " " 'Now,' " he confesses, " 'I think no longer of anything rude in my dreams, but the very last night we stayed in the garrison, I imagined I had a cabin in a grove of sugar maples, and at the root of every tree was a Mabel Dunham, while the birds that were among the branches sang ballads, instead of the notes that natur' gave, and even the deer stopped to listen' " (302).

When Natty recognizes that forest pleasures have " 'lost their charms' " (302) for him, he makes the fatal mistake of attempting to actualize his fantasy. In a conversation with Jasper Western, he announces that " 'Mabel and I intend to dwell in a cabin of our own, . . . [in] a beautiful spot about fifty miles west of the garrison that I had chosen in my mind, for my own place of abode' " (489–90). But in Cooper's world, sites chosen for forest seclusion and solitude do not convert into Edens. Woman and the woods answer the same needs, as Natty appears to recognize when he says, " 'natur' seems to have made them on purpose to sing in our ears when the music of the woods is silent!' " (499). But they exist in a mutually exclusive relationship, and when Jasper Western finally wins Mabel, he must take her away to civilization, her proper domain.

Jasper, like Ben, has emerged from the childhood world of the woods he and Natty had inhabited together, and this emergence necessitates a giving up of forest pleasures. Wom-

an, in this respect, means the intrusion of the adult (of
sexuality and responsibility). For Mabel to remain in the woods
would be to convert them into an adult realm, thus depriving
them of their magic (this is precisely what settlement building
does). Natty cannot be allowed to marry because he is Cooper's
one permanent link to the world of childhood, a figure whose
mind "was almost infantine in its simplicity and nature."
Pathfinder, Cooper tells us, is "a mere child: unpractised in the
ways of the world, he had no idea of concealing a thought of
any kind, and his mind received and reflected each emotion
with the pliability and readiness of that period of life" (304). It
is in this sense more than any other that Natty is an emanation
of the landscape; for he is a personification of the spirit of
childhood and inhabits the forest-world of childhood imagination.

It is true that in *The Deerslayer* Natty is initiated in a convincing manner (the scene in which he first takes a human life). Yet,
while we accept this initiation as real, its truth is formal rather
than psychological. Deerslayer is the same figure of "childish
simplicity" (416) after this event as he was before. He remains
essentially premature[16] and thereby becomes an embodiment,
or abstraction, of childhood—a character whose development
has been arrested so that he may always provide Cooper (and
the reader) with a way back to the world of the Glimmerglass.
And just as he denies himself marriage in *The Deerslayer*,
Cooper must deny it to him in *The Pathfinder*.

But while in psychological terms woman and the woods are
mutually exclusive objects of desire, aesthetically they are
mutually enhancing. When looked at in this way, the image of
woman can be seen to function in the same fashion as every
other significant metaphor in Cooper's descriptions. The
forest idyll cannot incorporate the presence of a real woman

16. There is a strain of criticism which finds Natty's childlike qualities
objectionable. For example, see Robert H. Zoellner's discussion of Leatherstocking's "infantile regressiveness" ("Conceptual Ambivalence in Cooper's
Leatherstocking," pp. 403, 418). But such infantilism, as Leslie Fiedler
suggests in a different context, is related to "the very essence of Cooper's appeal"
(*Love and Death*, p. 181).

any more than pristine nature can absorb a real te settlement. But as a way of seeing nature and investing human meaning, all of these images are felicitous.

Much has been written on the "wooden" quality of Cooper's females and on the degree to which they seem out of place in wilderness settings. But if we begin with the premise that the writer's talents and intentions were descriptive and pictorial, then character becomes subordinate to, even an aspect of, scene. Leatherstocking and certain other mythic heroes in Cooper's fiction have received the benefit of this explanation, but his women have not been granted the same apology, and with some justification. Yet, despite the familiar objections of modern readers, Cooper himself did not feel that his female characters were obtrusive elements in a natural landscape. To the contrary, he regarded them as essential aspects of the setting, a complement to the beauty of nature. In dozens of entries in his European travel journals, we can find passages such as this one: "The flats are covered with Maize, hemp, meadows and orchards, and the mountains, with vineyards— Very little grain—Women tambouring under the trees. Fine faces, delicate for their situation in life, and the forms slighter than in the Oberland" (*L&J*, 1: 302). For Cooper, women were as much a part of scenery as ruined castles and picturesque sunsets.

Female characters decorate the landscape in all of the forest tales, but the best example of the aesthetic relationship between woman and nature is *The Deerslayer*, a book which plays continually upon the mutual loveliness of the woods and of Judith Hutter. Throughout the novel, Judith's striking beauty is evoked by means of nature imagery: "Her rich hair shaded her spirited and yet soft countenance, even at that hour rendering it the more beautiful—as the rose is loveliest when reposing amid the shadows and contrasts of its native foliage" (97). Our first glimpse of her comes as she emerges from "an opening in the leaves" (62), suggesting the complementary aesthetic role she is to play.

One of Cooper's techniques is to heighten the beauty of nature by contrast. Judith is the loveliest of women imaginable, but she cannot compare to the loveliness of nature. An important motif of the novel is the continuing contrast of her "articles of dress" (165) with the natural "finery" of the woods, and although the former are inferior because they are artificial, the same is true of all the forms Cooper uses to articulate his vision of nature. Thus it is not so significant that Judith is tainted, for Natty would have chosen the woods as his "sweetheart" (146), as he tells Judith, regardless of the identity of the woman. In his eyes, nature is the fairer, purer bride, and he chooses her for the same reasons that he chooses the natural temple of the forest over the church in the settlement.

Of course, the female identification of nature goes deeper than Cooper's use of selected metaphors. His woods are pervasively feminine because of the enclosure, protection, and sustenance they provide. We have seen how both house and forest in Cooper's work reverberate the interiority of a feminine presence, and his novels illustrate Paul Shepard's point that, psychologically, "architecture and land forms are a continuum, an interlocked series entangled with the body image."[17] Cooper's woods contain many of the land forms Freud identified with the dream symbolism of the female body,[18] and it is important to maintain in the background of our thinking an awareness of the erotic properties of landscape. At this point, however, we are more interested in the image or "essence" of femininity than we are in psychoanalytic explanations.

In the final chapter of *The Oak Openings*, we make what seems to be a minor geographical discovery. As the narrator visits western Michigan thirty-six years after the events of the novel, he strolls through the " 'island' of forest" that lies in the middle of Prairie Round. "In the center of this wood," he comes upon "a little lake, circular in shape, and exceeding a quarter of a mile in diameter" (494). Cooper's placement of this body of water at the exact center of the novel's geography is apparently

17. *Man in the Landscape*, p. 100. Also see Annette Kolodny, *The Lay of the Land,* for a treatment of the female identification of landscape in the works of several early American writers, including Cooper.

18. Sigmund Freud, "Symbolism in Dreams," in *A General Introduction to Psycho-Analysis,* pp. 133–50.

gratuitous, a mere decoration—until we recognize that there was a lake at the center of his imagination.

That lake was of course Otsego, the Glimmerglass of *The Deerslayer*. This most vibrant image of centralized and concentrated solitude in all of Cooper's fiction is the ultimate forest enclosure. Encircled by a "belt of forest which inclosed it" (83), it exists as "a world by itself" (157). With its surrounding hills "clothed in the richest forest verdure" and its surface "glittering like a gem," the Glimmerglass appears to be "lighted up with a sort of radiant smile" (156). "The whole scene," Cooper writes, "was radiant with beauty" (135). This is "the pristine world of Glimmerglass" that Lawrence said was perhaps "lovelier than any place created in language."[19]

The setting of *The Deerslayer* illustrates Cooper's tendency to gravitate imaginatively toward a valued center-point bounded by a series of concentric circles. The mountains and forest enclose the Glimmerglass, and the lake surrounds the castle, which in turn contains its treasure. But the lake itself is the greatest treasure, a "gem of the forest" (595) which in every important way is the center of Cooper's imaginative geography.

In the narrowest sense the Glimmerglass is the center because, like a clearing, it organizes all the space around it by providing perspective. As the narrator tells us, "this was the first lake Deerslayer had ever seen. Hitherto, his experience had been limited to the courses of rivers and smaller streams, and never before had he seen so much of that wilderness which he so well loved, spread before his gaze" (110–11). Viewing the scene from the perspective of a canoe on the Glimmerglass, Deerslayer observes, " 'the lake seems made to let us get an insight [in-sight] into the noble forests' " (35). The lake, then, is nature's "eye," opening a view to all that surrounds it.

But the Glimmerglass is an eye in another sense too, for on its mirrorlike surface it represents, "contemplates," the world by reflection.[20] The trees and sky above are " 'cast upward

19. In the original version of "Fenimore Cooper's Leatherstocking Novels," written for the *English Review* and contained in *The Symbolic Meaning*; see p. 106.

20. In *L'eau et les rêves*, Bachelard writes, "A lake is a great tranquil eye. A

from its face; as if it would throw back the hills that hang over
it' " (44). This last observation is made by Harry March, who
perceives the loveliness of the lake but thinks "more of the
beauties of Judith Hutter than of those of the Glimmerglass"
(46). This is not true of Deerslayer who is entranced, almost
transfixed, by this wonder of nature that is "as smooth as glass
and as limpid as pure air" (45). For Leatherstocking, the
Glimmerglass radiates an absolute purity. As he gazes, he
becomes Bachelard's "dreamer of still water"; he experiences
"a communication of purity." "How one would wish,"
Bachelard writes, "to begin his life all over, a life which would
be the life of original dreams! Every reverie has a past, a distant
past and, for certain souls, the water reverie is privileged with
simplicity." [21]

As Bachelard says, the image of still water returns certain
souls to their origins, and if the forest is Deerslayer's
"sweetheart," there is reason to believe that the lake is his
"mother." A "beautiful basin" (171) of protective and enveloping substance, it has strong associations with the womb.
Throughout the narrative, the lake, and particularly "the
centre of the lake," is represented as the only "place of safety"
(343) in the novel's geography. When Cooper places a "house"
in the middle of this body of water, he is merging two of the
great, closely related, oneiric images in his fiction, for both the
castle and the Glimmerglass are enclosures which radiate an
intense feminine presence. Deerslayer's entering of the room
of the sisters brings to his mind "a rush of childish recollec-
tions. . . . He bethought him of his mother" (42). [22] The
former mistress of the castle, Judith's and Hetty's mother, now
lies dead at the bottom of the lake, and her mysterious, lingering presence pervades both realms. Cooper achieves this effect

---

lake absorbs all the light and makes a world of it. The world is already
contemplated, already represented by the lake" (*On Poetic Imagination and
Reverie*, p. 77). Cf. Thoreau on the lake as "earth's eye" (*Walden*, p. 186), and
Thomas Cole's comparison of the "unrippled lake" to an "eye in the human
countenance" ("Essay on American Scenery," p. 6).

21. *The Poetics of Reverie*, pp. 198–99.

22. In this room, Deerslayer also thinks "of a sister" (42). In the early
Cooperstown years, a beloved sister, Hannah, cared for the young Cooper
children, including James.

partly through Hetty's repeated, yearning questions about her dead parent, and it is the dull-witted but sentient Hetty who alone knows the location of the grave: "she often paddled a canoe, about sunset, or by the light of the moon, to the place, and gazed down into the limpid water, in the hope of being able to catch a glimpse of a form that she had so tenderly loved from infancy to the sad hour of their parting" (153).

The moonlight by which Hetty sometimes seeks her mother's burial place is only one of the nocturnal images of the novel. Even more evocative is the reflected light of stars, marking out a lustrous and beautiful "stripe of water" which plays across the exact center of the lake and points directly to the safety of the castle. This strange, reflected light resembles "a sort of inverted milky-way" (171). Bachelard observes that "a great number of poets, inspired by a serene vision, tell us of the milky beauty of a peaceful moonlit lake," and his analysis of the image helps to explain the magic of the Glimmerglass: "It is the image of a warm and happy night, the image of a clear and enveloping matter. An image which includes air and water, sky and earth, and unites them"; "it recalls the most ancient well-being, the sweetest of foods."[23]

How different the serene Glimmerglass is from Cooper's great ocean, or even from his great lake, Ontario. Where the Glimmerglass is surrounded by pine-covered hills, a world absolutely self-contained, the ocean is boundless, virtually infinite. While Cooper's description of the lake suggests a condensation of space—"it resembled a bed of the pure mountain atmosphere, compressed into a setting of hills and woods" (32–33)—his ocean throws us outward into horizontal immensity. The lake at its most strikingly beautiful is perfectly still and silent, the image of utter serenity and "deep repose" (45). The ocean, at its grandest, is thunderous, violent, awesome. And while the lake offers itself as a protection against adverse forces, the ocean is man's most dangerous combatant. For Natty Bumppo, Ontario, with its seemingly boundless extent, is the equivalent of an ocean. In *The Pathfinder*, he compares it to " 'a quick-tempered man, sudden to be angered, and as soon

23. *On Poetic Imagination and Reverie*, p. 60.

appeased' " (310). As I indicated earlier, the world of the sea (and prairie) has a strong masculine identification in Cooper's work. He seems to have associated the sudden "wrath" and force of the ocean with masculine energy (*animus*), whereas he felt the deep repose (*anima*) of the forest as a feminine presence.

Cooper's biography is helpful here, because it tells us that his experience with the ocean came in adolescence and young manhood, a time of great ferment and rebellion (which in his case resulted in expulsion from college—an event which led to his going to sea).[24] It may be that literary taste and convention do not entirely explain the fact that the heroes of Cooper's nautical romances are sexually charged, Byronic figures, who require the broadest possible field of action (the sea) to test their own limits and the limits of law and authority. (Compare the "penetrating" vision of the Pilot and the Red Rover to Leatherstocking's innocent eye.) We sometimes forget that Natty Bumppo is not an explorer or an adventurer, at least not in the same way as Cooper's nautical heroes are.[25] He leads the westward movement only by default, for he is forced out of his beloved woods, the "garden" in which he would have remained forever if that had been possible. Natty, like Ben Boden, is a child of the forest, and the settings these two characters inhabit answer to the deepest needs of childhood.

To discover the imaginative roots of a book like *The Deerslayer*, we must follow Bachelard's advice and "go beyond the time of fevers [adolescence] to find the tranquil time, the time of the happy childhood."[26] Edith Cobb has identified a period of development she calls "the little-understood, prepubertal, halcyon, middle age of childhood [defined by Freud as the stage of sexual latency], approximately from five

24. After expulsion from Yale at the age of seventeen, Cooper took service for a year aboard an American merchantman, the *Stirling*. Later he served aboard two naval vessels, the *Vesuvius* and the *Wasp*.

25. Except in *The Last of the Mohicans*, where he is characterized as possessing "that secret love of desperate adventure, which had increased with his experience, until hazard and danger had become, in some measure, necessary to the enjoyment of his existence" (289). For this, and other exceptional qualities of *The Last of the Mohicans*, see part 3.

26. *The Poetics of Reverie*, p. 110.

or six to eleven or twelve—between the strivings of animal infancy and the storms of adolescence—when the natural world is experienced in some highly evocative way, producing . . . a sense of some profound continuity with natural processes." The age span of this privileged time of life, during which we develop our spirit of place, corresponds to the period of the writer's childhood in Cooperstown. And although we have little specific knowledge of that childhood,[27] the novels tell us all we need to know. Natty Bumppo is surely the child within Cooper, and his adventures in the woods objectify the primal impressions and experiences of being in nature. The forest romances contain all those patterns of chase and escape and the seeking of refuge that express the child's need "to make a world in which to find a place to discover a self."[28] The places thus found and inhabited—the secret hiding places and other valued enclosures of our childhoods—become charged with meaning and remain intact in our memories as valued images to be reexperienced when we are adults.

To engage in such remembering can project us into a state of reverie, an experience not only pleasurable but necessary, for as Bachelard reminds us, reverie "helps us inhabit the world." To read Cooper makes us into daydreamers of the forest and "returns us to the beauty of the first images."[29] His fiction lends itself to this salutary experience for several reasons. To dream our own magic woods, we require a text which does not describe the space of nature in too much detail. We do not want to know the names of the flora and fauna (there is little to interest the naturalist in Cooper's fiction) but only to be presented with a beautiful outline, a matrix which touches deep places within our memories and then allows us to dream our own dreams. Cooper's works answer this need perfectly, for his descriptions

27. For the most detailed account we have, see Marcel Clavel, *Fenimore Cooper*, esp. chap. 2, "L'Enfance d'un fils de pionnier."

28. Edith Cobb, "The Ecology of Imagination in Childhood," pp. 538, 540. In the early Cooperstown years, Hannah Cooper wrote affectionately of her younger brothers, including James, "They are very wild and show plainly they have been bred in the woods" (*The Legends and Traditions of a Northern Country*, p. 171).

29. *The Poetics of Reverie*, pp. 22, 103.

are diffuse, inexact, generalized.[30] They present a high degree of "indeterminacy," a porous quality requiring the reader to fill in gaps in the prose "by a free play of meaning-projection."[31] This helps to explain why illustrations of Cooper's fiction, whether drawn in his time or ours, often take us so completely by surprise. Although language is generally a more porous medium than paint or engraving, it is especially true of this novelist that we find in his descriptions our own remembered landscapes, landscapes necessarily different from those depicted by the illustrator.

In *The Poetics of Reverie*, Bachelard makes a distinction between daydream and nightdream. The latter, he says, "does not belong to us. It is not of our possession" (145). In the nightdream, we sometimes feel that someone else is forcing us into regions where we do not want to go. Daydreams (reverie), on the other hand, are our absolute possession. In the active and conscious experience of daydreaming, we move into areas of our own choosing, ultimately creating a whole cosmos that belongs to us. One could argue that the visions of nature rendered by Brockden Brown, Poe, and Hawthorne are examples of nightdream. These writers often create worlds which seem out of control, worlds constantly changing shape for the characters and the reader. Often with Poe, and sometimes with Hawthorne, as in "Young Goodman Brown," the nightdream becomes a nightmare.

But Cooper's forest "holds still" for us. It makes reverie possible as it enables us to explore a world that is permanent and out of time. His vision of the wilderness is classic, classic in exactly the same way that childhood is a "permanent, durable immobile world." Cooper's timeless woods hold human action in the stasis of the classical drama and possess the formal beauty of the park and garden. And his most radiant image, that of the lake, awakens "our cosmic imagination through the beauty of a reflected world."[32]

30. See William C. Brownell, *American Prose Masters*, p. 11.
31. Wolfgang Iser, "Indeterminacy and the Reader's Response in Prose Fiction," in *Aspects of Narrative*, p. 12.
32. *The Poetics of Reverie*, pp. 20, 198.

PART III

The Landscape of Difficulty

I have great pleasure in seeing any descendant of my father in this house, for I think it would have given him pleasure to know that his posterity meet in this spot, where I should think they must be induced to think of its founder. I have embellished a little, but he founded the place, and it is the first man who becomes identified with any thing of this sort. I have had a good deal of difficulty in keeping possession, there being a very strong disposition in this country to make common property of any thing that takes the fancy of the public. I suppose one half of this village would gladly pull down this house, because they can not walk through the hall whenever it suits them; but I am firm, and they begin to feel that what is my property is not theirs.

Letters and Journals, 5: 369

6

Exploring the Neutral Ground

> Any one who is familiar with the aspect of things in what is
> called a "new country" in America, must be well aware it is
> not very inviting.
>
> *The Chainbearer*

A true phenomenology of the space of Cooper's imaginative
world must take account of *The Last of the Mohicans*. In many
ways, this adventure tale seems to violate the aesthetics of
landscape that inform and control his other forest novels. The
narrator begins to lay out the geography of the book on the
first page, where he stresses "the toils and dangers of the
wilderness" and explains the necessity of "struggling against
the rapids of the streams" and "effecting the rugged passes of
the mountains." Unlike *The Deerslayer*, where such terrain is
merely referred to and then left behind for the preferred
space of the interior (pastoral) forest, here the introductory
descriptions serve to prepare us for a journey through a landscape which becomes, to use Cooper's terms, increasingly
"broken," "interrupted," "ragged"—a landscape consistently
drawn in images of "difficulty" (11).

The unusual treatment of space in this work is most evident
at the level of the individual image. But if we step back to
examine the larger design of *The Last of the Mohicans*, we find at
that level too a striking peculiarity. Generally, Cooper's novels
possess highly structured and formal settings. In some, a dominant feature of the landscape acts as a moral center of
gravity and holds the action of the novel within a tightly
bounded perimeter, thereby creating a self-contained world

which draws its imaginative power from the qualities of stasis and centrality.

Both the first and last written of the Leatherstocking tales, *The Pioneers* and *The Deerslayer*, are ordered on such a spatial plan, and as distinct as the worlds of these two novels are, they demonstrate the same use of space to create meaning. The opening scenes of both novels show the characters traveling through a wooded landscape that overlies a mountain lake, but in each case the action shifts quickly to a well-defined "arena" that becomes the geographic and moral center of each work. In *The Deerslayer* this center is the lake itself, the Glimmerglass, a beautiful image of virgin nature that totally contains the world of the novel. In *The Pioneers* Judge Temple and his party descend through the woods toward the same lake, but in this work the central feature of the landscape is the community of Templeton. Much of the narrative is given over to a detailed description of the architectural and social forms of the community, thus holding our vision on the center, and in every other important way Templeton dominates the world of the novel and draws a circle of influence around the entire surrounding landscape. In the fullest sense, it is the reference point of the book. Even a character like Natty Bumppo who is identified with the woods must return to this center periodically, because it defines and dictates the terms of existence of the whole environment. *The Pioneers*, then, like *The Deerslayer*, creates a fully defined world of the imagination, locked in place and fixed in time (or out of time in the case of *The Deerslayer*) by the cohesive effect of a static and dominant center.

The Last of the Mohicans does not possess such a center. Its spatial meaning is not created by stasis and centrality; rather, the narrative seems to be ordered on the basis of constant motion. This in itself does not make it unique among Cooper's adventure tales. Several of the forest novels have a journey for their structure; a good example is *The Pathfinder*. At a glance, this romance seems to bear a close resemblance to *The Last of the Mohicans*. Both novels enact a hazardous journey through the wilderness to a fort commanded by the heroine's father. In each, the narrative holds the characters briefly at the scene of the fort and then moves them through space again into the even deeper wilderness. But anyone who has read both of these Leatherstocking tales knows that the analogy is superficial. The fact that Cooper ordered *The Pathfinder* on the principle of movement rather than stasis does not prevent him from developing in it some of the most strikingly beautiful pastoral images in his fiction. Like *The Deerslayer*, *The Pathfinder* creates a world full of hazard, but the context for danger is the dream-space of the idealized woods. Indeed, this mixture of danger and beauty is one of the most important defining characteristics of these two, last-written, of the Leatherstocking tales. Conversely, none of Cooper's forest novels is so devoid of pastoral space as is *The Last of the Mohicans*. Its danger and violence are answered not by images of tranquillity and beauty but by a landscape of austerity and difficulty.

Furthermore, in most of Cooper's journey novels, motion creates meaning by establishing a clear "direction" and a recognizable "objective." The journey often leads toward a human structure—a house, a fort, or a settlement—which is in need of defense against adverse forces. The climax of such novels occurs at the moment of attack, so that all the motions of journeying can be seen, in retrospect, to have prepared for this moment. After the structure is defended,[1] the mysteries of the plot unravel quickly and the novel concludes. The attack on the blockhouse and Leatherstocking's heroic defense of it (and Mabel Dunham) climax the action of *The Pathfinder*; these events decide the military confrontation, expose the villain, and allow the romantic triangle to be resolved. Similarly, the journey that structures the second half of *Satanstoe* leads toward the besieged settlement of Ravensnest. When Corny Littlepage and his party reach the settlement and successfully turn back the Indian attackers, the reader knows that all the

1. The structure is not always defended successfully. But even in those novels in which it is destroyed, the "direction" of the motion toward the valued structure (as well as the meaning of its destruction) is clear. For further discussion of threatened dwellings in Cooper's fiction, see chap. 9.

issues of the book will be resolved quickly. Civilization can now take hold in the wilderness; the values of Corny's (and Cooper's) class are affirmed; and Anneke Mordaunt reveals her love for the hero. All of these developments are related to one another, and they are all "released" in the climactic moments of the battle and its aftermath. The spatial "objective" in the journey novel is, then, closely related in function to the "center" in Cooper's novels of geographic stasis. In different ways, they both define the values to be defended in the world of the book, establish a comprehensible context for adventure and action, and order and compose the novel's geography.

Although *The Last of the Mohicans* at first seems to follow the usual journey pattern, we realize after only a few pages that our expectations will not be met. Instead of the predictable rhythms of travel and rest, acceleration and hesitation, conflict and tranquil observation of scene, we experience fits and bursts of motion, violent "interruption," and a "ragged" landscape that impedes a steady flow of movement through space. The journey does not lead to the successful defense of its "objective," Fort William Henry, for Leatherstocking and his party reach the fort only to see it destroyed and its inhabitants massacred in one of the most violent scenes in Cooper's fiction. And at this point in the novel, more than half the action remains to be narrated. If *The Last of the Mohicans* possesses a significant spatial pattern, it is of a very different kind than exists elsewhere in his fiction.

The eccentric qualities of this book have not gone unnoticed. In the most recent important contribution to discussion of the novel, Thomas Philbrick reviews previous attempts to categorize and explain *The Last of the Mohicans* and finds them all deficient. Focusing upon the discordant sound images and the violence, he argues that earlier interpretations break down when subjected to an intense examination of the novel's imagery. He says that attempts to find meaning and structure in *The Last of the Mohicans* are futile because all such readings ask questions of the book which are "inappropriate and hence incapable of yielding conclusive answers." "Such questions," he continues, "presuppose the existence of conscious intellectual control by the novelist over the materials of his fiction and assume that those materials are ordered in an ideological scheme which, once identified, will unlock the meaning of the book."[2]

Philbrick has performed a valuable service, for he has made impossible, henceforth, those familiar readings that impose interpretations based upon the standard formulas of analysis. But the problem with his essay is that, having obliterated all patterns and meanings that others have found in the book, he supplies nothing in their place which could constitute a full interpretation. For him, the meaning of the book is chaos itself, and *The Last of the Mohicans* is an example of pure gothicism, a journey through a "landscape of nightmare"[3] in which nothing is certain except the certainty of "discord." Perhaps the difficulty lies in his assumption that the only way artistic order is achieved is by the imposition of "conscious intellectual control." One could argue that many of Cooper's most power-ful effects result from some ordering principle deeper than conscious intent. But for whatever reasons, Philbrick's reading is, finally, unconvincing. Not only is it hard to imagine Cooper writing such a novel (Philbrick argues that a case of feverish sunstroke played a part in producing the aberration), but it is hard to imagine any writer creating a work so utterly detached from the body of his fiction. In fact, *The Last of the Mohicans* is not *sui generis*. The very qualities that make it, as Philbrick says, "profoundly different in nature from Cooper's other fiction,"[4] are paradoxically the same qualities that link it firmly to the writer's world. Published in 1826, this was Cooper's sixth novel, and it can be understood best as the culmination of his early work; it is, as we shall see, the book that sets the direction for all that he will do subsequently. Although there is no comparable tale of wilderness adventure among the five novels

2. "*The Last of the Mohicans* and the Sounds of Discord," p. 25.
3. "Sounds of Discord," p. 40.
4. "Sounds of Discord," p. 25.

preceding it, all the issues that force their way to eruption in
this violent work, even the elements that comprise its landscape, can be found in the novels of this early period.

In many of his works, Cooper depicts a zone of intermediate
space which lies between well-defined areas of the setting. In
The Deerslayer, for example, Leatherstocking becomes mired
and is captured in the "low marshy land that intervened"
(155) between the distinct worlds of lake and forest. During the
early period this kind of terrain tends to dominate Cooper's
fiction, and the geography of one of these novels is almost
totally constituted of the broken images of intermediate space.
As the subtitle of *The Spy* (1821) indicates, this *Tale of the Neutral
Ground* is set in an essentially ambiguous geography positioned
between the British and American held territories above New
York City during the Revolution. But the historical situation is
less important to us at this point than the characteristics of the
setting, for the neutral ground of *The Spy*—Cooper's second
novel and the first of his American novels[5]—is the model for
the landscape of difficulty wherever it appears in his work.
It has often been observed that Cooper's fictional use of
neutral ground derives from the work of Sir Walter Scott. For
both Cooper and Scott, neutral ground implies an area beyond
the safe limits of civilized life where the hero is tested by
dangerous foes and by the environment. A region of rapid
change, it is inhabited by representatives of at least two warring
factions, neither of whom control it.[6] But of more importance

5. I begin this survey of Cooper's early works with *The Spy* rather than
Precaution (his first novel) because the latter is a highly imitative novel of
manners set in England, a work which sheds little light upon the matter of
landscape.

6. For example, see George Dekker, *James Fenimore Cooper the Novelist*, pp.
33–34; Leslie A. Fiedler, *Love and Death*, pp. 179, 186–87; Edwin Fussell,
Frontier, pp. 11–18. In his recent study of Cooper, John P. McWilliams, Jr.,
emphasizes the aspect of change in the neutral ground. He extends the
application of the term to include the settings of all Cooper's American novels,
arguing that all "are laid in a time of social change." He continues, "Cooper
may place his characters in Connecticut, on the prairie, or on a Pacific island,

than any of this for Cooper is the fact that the neutral ground is not *possessed*. It is a landscape full of change because no one has fully appropriated and defined it. Aesthetically, it is neutral space because it possesses neither the perfect design of virgin wilderness nor the design art gives to space appropriated for the highest forms and uses of civilization. Neutral ground is related to the condition that Cooper, in a letter to his wife, called "the raw look of a new region" (*L&J*, 5:45), referring to those parts of America that had not yet emerged from the unattractive settlement stage of development. The crucial factor is that the neutral ground lacks demarcations; it exhibits neither the "curved lines" that order nature nor the design of civilized space. Further, it is a territory without law, and law is the moral equivalent of geographic demarcation. In the landscape of difficulty, neither legal nor geographic boundary has any certain meaning. In such a region, it is impossible to know the boundaries between nature and civilization, between the territories of one warring group and another, and at the deepest level, between "mine" and "not mine."

We know that the "middle," regardless of the area of conceptualization, was deeply problematical for Cooper. Just as he valued both primitive man (the Indian) and the landed gentry but distrusted America's emerging middle class, he could become profoundly disturbed over any state of being which was not clearly "here" or "there." In his work, the "middle" is always identified with lack of control and potential chaos. For this reason, the space of the neutral ground is the most threatening and dangerous landscape in his fictional world.

but they all inhabit a single setting—constant in its fluidity." "Characters are caught," he says, "not only in a time that gives them little fixity, but in a place that affords them less" (*Political Justice in a Republic*, pp. 6, 7–8). But this reading does not take account of the aesthetic differences among Cooper's works. As I show in part 4, several of the writer's most important novels create a tightly bounded world immune to the intrusion of change and history. Donald Ringe accurately defines the neutral ground as a "physical and moral no-man's-land," but he too applies the term much too broadly, identifying the landscape of *The Spy* with "the forest or the Great Plains in the Leatherstocking tales and the sea in *The Pilot*" (*James Fenimore Cooper*, p. 28).

And in early novels such as *The Spy,* Cooper seems to have found it necessary to explore this region in order to·come to terms with it.

The landscape of *The Spy* is rendered in images of terrible difficulty, a characteristic which objectifies the writer's uneasiness with states of ambiguity: "For two hours more they struggled with the difficult and dangerous passes of the Highlands, without road, or any other guide than the moon" (425). The moral obscurity of the neutral ground is symbolized by visual obscurity, and several of the important scenes (such as the one above) are set at night. The dominant spatial quality is that of obstacle and interruption. Unlike the easy flow of movement afforded by the "leafy corridors" of Cooper's interior forest, the landscape of difficulty obstructs visual perception and impedes physical movement. Strewn with "scattered trees and fantastic rocks" (338), it makes any kind of human activity based upon order, especially military operations, problematical: "Dunwoodie, who was severely, but not dangerously wounded, recalled his men from further attempts, which, in that stony country, must necessarily be fruitless" (448). In such a setting, frustration mounts quickly and anger flares against " 'Those cursed rocks!' " (327).

Pastoral novels such as *The Deerslayer* idealize the climate of the North American woods and are usually set in the spring or summer of the year. In *The Spy,* the season reflects the moral uncertainty and unpredictability of life in the neutral ground: "The weather, which had been mild and clear since the storm, now changed with the suddenness of the American climate." "Towards evening," Cooper relates, "the cold blasts poured down from the mountains, and flurries of snow plainly indicated that the month of November had arrived; a season whose temperature varies from the heats of summer to the cold of winter" (206). The "unstable climate" of *The Spy* changes "with the rapid transitions of magic" (246) and corresponds to the novel's pervasive atmosphere of difficulty and unpredictability.

In *The Spy,* the ambiguity that defines the environment also characterizes the human realm. The hero, Harvey Birch, is a master of disguise who changes identity frequently, who appears and disappears with uncanny timeliness, and who negotiates "the imperfect culture of the neutral ground" (425) with a facility that seems supernatural. In the elusive reality that is the world of the novel, nothing is certain, nothing "holds." Those thought virtuous are revealed as corrupt; the loyal are found treacherous. Here is a setting in which anything can happen. The Skinners, those archetypal marauders of Cooper's imagination, thrive in such an environment. These outlaws pretend allegiance to the American side but use the war as a pretext for acts of murder and plunder. They represent the underside of revolution, the greed and violence that surface in times of trouble alongside the obvious nobility and courage of a figure like Harper (George Washington). The Skinners prefigure all the other marauders in Cooper's fiction, such as the "redskins" of the novel of that title—men who totally ignore the sanctity of boundaries and ownership.

But the Skinners are merely exploiting a larger conflict, and while Cooper finds it easy to condemn their activities, his attitude toward the conflict itself is much more complicated. It is no accident that of his first five novels, three deal directly with the American War of Independence. Cooper seems to have regarded the Revolution as the event which, though necessary, had introduced into American life the full force of history and had thereby set into motion dangerous, potentially uncontrollable, forces.[7] More than this, it symbolized for him the primary conflict of his imagination, the struggle between authority and freedom and, more profoundly, between the claims of the father and the rights of the son. At the deepest level, this is what makes the neutral ground so "difficult." Here are the claims that most need to be settled, and here is the line of demarcation that most needs to be fixed.

The space of Cooper's fiction objectifies his own "interior."

7. For a political interpretation of Cooper's ambivalence to the Revolution, see McWilliams, chap. 1. Also see my essay, "A Repossession of America."

In the revolutionary war novels, the primary "forces" of his imagination are symbolized by British authority and American rebellion. On one level, *The Spy* is the least equivocal of these works, for in it the spirit of rebellion is safely embodied in America's most revered father-figure, George Washington. But Cooper's landscapes are always the truest measure of the spiritual climate of his novels, and the landscape of *The Spy* reveals the sense of uncertainty with which he approached his subject.

In *The Pilot* (1824), Cooper's ambivalence is much more apparent. John Paul Jones's passionate hatred of British authority, a hatred which derives from an undisclosed but unforgivable indignity " 'suffered from his own countrymen' " (486), leads him to join the revolutionary forces in the War of Independence. As we saw earlier, Cooper admires and celebrates the courage and skill of the Pilot but distrusts his turbulent inner life. Jones is characterized by "wild ambition" (421), and it is suggested that his " 'devotion to America proceeded from desire of distinction, his ruling passion' " (486). Cooper seems, at least partially, to endorse the following denunciation of revolution made by the novel's obvious authority figure, a British aristocrat named Colonel Howard: " 'Rebellion pollutes all that it touches. . . . Although it commences under the sanction of holy liberty, it ever terminates in despotism' " (149). As if to confirm Howard's prophecy, we discover at the conclusion of the novel that although the Pilot " 'commenced his deeds in the cause of these free States, they terminated in the service of a despot!' " (486).

Ultimately, the novel affirms the ideals of the Revolution and approves the American destiny (even Colonel Howard acknowledges the justness of the American cause on his deathbed), but not without first drawing into serious question the motives that generate political rebellion. The geography of *The Pilot* objectifies Cooper's ambivalence. In his fiction, the sea symbolizes freedom while architectural structures on land tend to represent established order and tradition; but this novel never quite decides between these realms. For a nautical tale, *The Pilot* is exceedingly land-bound; the two American ships never range beyond sight of the coast, and more than half the action of the novel takes place on land.[8]

The American sailors, nevertheless, are closely identified by their "wild" natures with the ocean from which they come to raid the British coastline. The spatial objective of the mission is Colonel Howard's home, an ancient manor house named St. Ruth's Abbey which clearly symbolizes England's established order. But between these two antagonistic realms lies an area of neutral ground, the "difficult passes of the seashore" (203) on which much of the action takes place. When the American sailors enter this "rugged and dangerous" (28) area, they find it "full of rocks, and sandpits, and shoals" (16). As in *The Spy*, they voice their discontent as they perform the "difficult task of ascending the rocks" (19). This "hard-featured landscape" (29) is neither land nor sea, and its essential ambiguity identifies it immediately as a landscape of difficulty. Here, representatives of different worlds clash by night in a fog-ridden and "threatening atmosphere" (17) which obscures all perception. Violence and confusion dominate this murky setting in which no one's true identity is certain. Later in the decade of the 1820s, Cooper would write a nautical tale (*The Red Rover*, 1827) which would unequivocally celebrate wild freedom, and appropriately, all of the important action would take place on the open sea. But *The Pilot* shows that, in this earlier period, the landscape of difficulty continued to claim a large portion of the writer's interior geography.

Perhaps Cooper is able to advance the cause of the rebel-hero as far as he does in *The Pilot* because Byron (and to a lesser degree, Scott) had effectively popularized the Noble Outlaw for American readers. But from another point of view the

8. Thomas Philbrick sees this "reluctance to leave the shore" as a reflection of Cooper's failure "to have developed in *The Pilot* the complete and consistent conception of the meaning of the sea that informs its successors" (*James Fenimore Cooper and the Development of American Sea Fiction*, pp. 53–54).

Byronic sanction was inhibiting, for this nautical romance is so heavy with romantic convention that the rebellion of the central character strikes us today as stylized and "literary."

A far more authentic rebellion takes place in another of the early novels, one which draws its power from Cooper's own childhood experience. Henry Nash Smith has tantalizingly written of *The Pioneers* (1823): "When an author turns to autobiographical material of this sort and introduces a central character resembling his father, one does not have to be very much of a Freudian to conclude that the imagination is working on a deeper level than usual." We might question whether the imagination is working on a deeper level in *The Pioneers* than it is in several other works in which the same conflict appears, but Smith is correct in identifying certain characteristics of civilization with the father. He argues that "all the aspects of authority—institutional stability, organized religion, class stratification, property—are exhibited as radiating from the symbol of the father." "But," Smith continues, "if the father rules, and rules justly, it is still true that in this remembered world of his childhood Cooper figures as the son. Thus he is able to impart real energy to the statement of the case for defiance and revolt."[9]

But this too needs qualification, for Judge Marmaduke Temple is not a Colonel Howard. He does not represent established tradition but instead asserts an untried and crude authority which threatens previously established rights. This is the profound reversal that Cooper works in *The Pioneers*, for in the novel, the "father" becomes the usurper of the ancient claims of the "son." Temple, we learn, has acquired his wilderness lands by "purchasing estates that had been wrested by violence [in the Revolution] from others," those long-established families whose sympathy with the British had caused them to lose all their American holdings. Temple is thus subtly identified with the dark and rapacious underside of revolution, and though the novel's tidy conclusion disassociates

9. *Virgin Land,* pp. 67, 68.

him from such forces (he had protected the Effingham estate from revolutionary factions), Cooper's characterization is a little less than subtle: "While . . . he discharged his functions with credit and fidelity, Marmaduke never seemed to lose sight of his own interests." The narrator calls this acquisitiveness but a "slight stain" (36) on Temple's character, but our suspicions have been raised to the point that the accusation of Oliver (Edwards) Effingham—he believes the Judge is guilty of land theft—seems to have moral, if not legal, basis. As the descendant of the dispossessed Effingham family, Oliver is the true representative of civilization in the novel. Marmaduke Temple, whose primary motive in establishing Templeton has been "to accumulate wealth" (255), is a civilization builder, which is quite another thing.

Cooper's treatment of the Judge shows great ambivalence. Temple proclaims his intention to preserve the natural resources of the wilderness, yet in both the pigeon-shoot and the fish-kill, he can be seen "yielding to the excitement of the moment" (284) and forgetting "the morality of Leather-stocking" (273).[10] He is carefully distinguished from his more thoughtless agents such as Hiram Doolittle and Richard Jones, yet Cooper leaves little doubt that these men work his will. Doolittle is a "callous architect" (362) who also practices specious law, thus personifying two of the imperfect structures of the "middle" stage of civilization. The image of Natty Bumppo imprisoned in Templeton's crude jail links the town's architecture with the arbitrariness of its makeshift legal system.

The destructive settlement stage of development brings about the imposition of the straight line upon the natural "curved lines" of nature (high civilization brings a return of the

10. As several critics have pointed out, Leatherstocking himself yields to temptation when he kills the swimming buck. Yet this act is very different in quality from the pigeon-shoot and the fish-kill, which have nothing of the spirit of the hunt about them. Natty's act identifies him with an earlier period when the relation between hunter and animal was defined by ecological balance and by what Gary Snyder calls "Hunting magic" (*Earth House Hold,* p. 120). Also see Paul Shepard on "fellow creatures" (*Man in the Landscape,* chap. 6).

curve), and it has been Richard Jones's responsibility to lay out "the streets and *blocks* . . . [of] a city" (106). Jones, heedless of the ecological hazards of the grid, tells Elizabeth Temple, " 'We must run our streets by the compass, coz, and disregard trees, hills, ponds, stumps, or, in fact, anything but prosperity. Such is the will of your father' " (199).[11] It is fitting that Elizabeth questions the wisdom of such planning, for woman in Cooper is always identified with the beauty of the natural world. As Bachelard says, "the angle is masculine and the curve feminine." "Space that has been seized upon by the imagination," he writes, "cannot remain indifferent space subject to the measures and estimates of the surveyor. It has been lived in . . . with all the partiality of the imagination."[12]

Elizabeth has come to the crude pioneer community from a world of refinement, and this too is appropriate because in Cooper's work woman mediates between the natural pastoral of the wilderness and the civilized pastoral of fully developed cultures. In this "middle" stage Elizabeth seems out of place, and it is through her eyes that we make our first significant tally of Templeton's past beauty and its present "incongruity" (46): "time was given Elizabeth to dwell on a scene which was so rapidly altering under the hands of man, that it only resembled, in its outlines, the picture she had so often studied with delight, in childhood" (40).

This lost world of childhood is the world Natty Bumppo would like to reclaim. In the attempt, he has become, in the eyes of Richard Jones, " 'a kind of outlaw' " (391). But his claim to possession of the landscape clearly antedates that of Judge Temple. When Temple first looked out upon these lands from the pinnacle of Mount Vision, he saw smoke coming from Natty's " 'rough cabin of logs' " (259), a primitive structure

11. Temporally, too, the settlement is in conflict with nature. As Natty is departing at the novel's conclusion, he tells Elizabeth and Oliver that he organizes his life according to natural rhythms of necessity, while they regard time in a different sense: " 'I eat when hungry, and drink when a-dry; and ye keep stated hours and rules' " (503).

12. *The Poetics of Space,* pp. 146, xxxii.

which existed before the present unsightly buildings of Templeton were conceived. And long before Temple's arrival,
" 'when the tract was first surveyed [the initial, conceptual,
imposition of the straight line], under the Indian grant' "
(169), Natty had even then resided in the woods.

The most ancient claims are of course those of the Indian,
represented in this novel by Indian John, whom Natty calls the
" 'right owner' " (170) of the land. It is rumored among the
townspeople that Oliver is the half-breed son of Chingachgook, and although this is not true, these two figures are
"related." For the Delawares had long ago deeded in council
the lands around Templeton to Oliver's grandfather, Major
Effingham, and the claims of Oliver and Indian John are
thus united.[13] In Cooper's imagination, the natural nobility of
the Indian is associated with the refinement of high culture,
and in this novel, the primitive and the civilized are organized
against the usurping "middle."

But the lesson of *The Pioneers* is that while Oliver's claim will
be made good those of Natty and Indian John will not. John
must die in the forest fire, and Leatherstocking must depart.
Time cannot be reversed, for as Elizabeth knows, it is impossible to " 'convert these clearings and farms again into hunting-
grounds, as the Leather-stocking would wish to see them' "
(308). Cooper's response to this reality principle is not overtly
bitter but is instead careful and ironic. His tone is one of
restrained but defensive "laughter," an indication of his need
to distance himself from the world he creates.

In many ways, the setting of *The Pioneers* corresponds to the
landscape of difficulty that is so prominent in the geography of
Cooper's early works. The "changeful country" (236) of the
novel is rendered in images of confusion and "deformity" (46),
and even its woods contain few of the pastoral images that fill

13. Thomas Philbrick makes the important point that because Oliver is "the
grandson of Major Effingham, who had been proclaimed a chief by the
Delawares and adopted by Mohegan as a son, he is firmly linked to the Indian
past" ("Cooper's *The Pioneers*," p. 593). In *The Redskins*, the real Indians help to
defend the Ravensnest estate against the "redskins" (anti-rent forces).

the space of Cooper's later forest novels. Yet in one sense, this is not the true neutral ground, for the question of possession has been decided from the first page of the book. Though there is much bitter contention, there is no real contest, for, as Elizabeth recognizes, " 'The enterprise of Judge Temple is taming the very forests' " (232). Richard Jones's question of the Judge is merely rhetorical: " 'Do you not own the mountains as well as the valleys? Are not the woods your own?' " (99). The hope implicit in *The Pioneers* is that through the union of Elizabeth Temple and Oliver Effingham, Templeton may eventually become a true civilization no longer in conflict with the natural world.[14]

Cooper's ambivalent treatment of Marmaduke Temple, then, can be explained in these terms. The Judge is the father of civilization in the procreative sense of fathering. For Cooper, this is both an exciting and a potentially destructive role;[15] if abused, it can bring about the rape of the land. And the landscape of *The Pioneers* shows much evidence that it has been violated by the father/maker of civilizations. Cooper himself identified much more strongly with the Oliver Effingham figure, whose descendant, Edward (in *Home as Found*), assumes the role of father/protector rather than father/maker. This parallels Cooper's own role as the protector of the estate founded by his father in Cooperstown, a role he took very seriously. The protector of civilization's established structures and values is a gentleman, a man of culture and refinement

14. See Philbrick, "Cooper's *The Pioneers*," pp. 590–92.
15. Cooper's ambivalence is striking. He seems to have had an affectionate relationship with his father and admired him greatly. In *Wyandotté*, he expresses what must be read as an identification with his father's role as a maker of civilization: "There is a pleasure in diving into a virgin forest and commencing the labors of civilization, that has no exact parallel in any other human occupation. That of building, or of laying out grounds, has certainly some resemblance to it, but it is a resemblance so faint and distant as scarcely to liken the enjoyment each produces. The former approaches nearer to the feeling of creating" (42–43). Yet, as I have shown in part 2, the emphasis for Cooper fell on the artistic aspects of "creating." Cf. Fussell, p. 28.

(unlike his "pioneer" ancestor) who, not incidentally, is in a position to marry the Judge's daughter.

In the novel written immediately before *The Last of the Mohicans,* Cooper pushed this reversal to its furthest extreme. In *Lionel Lincoln* (1825), the son (this time it is a literal father-son relationship) stands on the side of order and tradition while the father is associated with violent and destructive rebellion. In this most troubled of the revolutionary war novels, Lionel Lincoln returns to colonial Boston, the city of his birth and childhood, as a British soldier sent by the Crown to stifle rebellion. As in *The Last of the Mohicans,* a historical event (the Battle of Bunker Hill) orders the narrative. Lionel, torn between loyalty to England and an impulse to join with the Americans, wanders in a state of disorientation through the novel's dark and violent landscape. The plot is too complex to summarize briefly, but it is sufficient to point out that *Lionel Lincoln* is Cooper's most thoroughly gothic work. It treats violence, disease, amputation, insanity (the hero's father is ultimately revealed to be a homicidal maniac), and imbecility—all of which are indirectly associated with the revolutionary fervor.[16] For Cooper, it is an incredibly dark and labyrinthine work of fiction.

The setting differs in some respects from the Highlands of *The Spy,* but it has all the essential characteristics of the neutral ground. Many of the scenes are nocturnal, and several are set in gloomy interiors; a storm rages out of control, and much of

16. Critics have objected to the ending of *Lionel Lincoln,* in which the character Ralph is revealed to be both a madman and Lionel's father. James Grossman sees it as a trick ending which ruins the novel (*James Fenimore Cooper,* p. 42). George Dekker agrees and adds, "I think we need not suppose that even subconsciously Cooper meant to suggest that there was a serious analogy to be drawn between the American Revolution and a madman's attempt to escape from an asylum" (p. 41), a judgment shared by John P. McWilliams, Jr. (p. 84). Yet, when we consider the novel in the general context of "difficulty" characteristic of all the works of this early period, I think we can indeed make such a supposition. Far from a trick, the ending, though a surprise, follows the deep logic of the narrative.

the action is shrouded in fog. Lionel's sleeping nightmares merge with his waking visions as he encounters a series of grotesque figures, most of whom he discovers are related to himself in a bizarre network of familial relations. At the conclusion, the hero and his bride flee the dangers and confusion of the new world for the safety and "clarity" of the old.

Lionel Lincoln is more than an experiment in gothicism,[17] but that is certainly part of its significance. It shows Cooper moving uncharacteristically into the region of nightmare, where distinctions between inner and outer worlds break down. In visual terms, this means that he was at least partially turning away from a representational treatment of landscape in favor of a more "symbolic," psychological mode. This slippage between reality and states of mind reflects a radical shortening of the narrative distance Cooper usually maintains between the world and the perceiving eye. In this novel, he gothicizes the already uncertain and difficult landscape of the neutral ground, and the visual confusion corresponds to the incestuous web of personal relations that Lionel uncovers in his quest for origins. It is possible the novel is Cooper's troubled search for his own (psychological) origins, but however that may be, the obvious artistic failure of the book demonstrates that he was not at home in the land of Brockden Brown and Poe. The gothic would have a place in his fiction, but only as an adjunct to his representationalism. Lionel Lincoln appears to be a novel written at a point of impasse; it probes the nightmarish regions of Cooper's inner landscape, but in doing so it dangerously obscures those "demarcations" that structure his world. The need now was to fight clear of the landscape of difficulty in order to establish more firmly the method and ideas of his art.

17. Lionel Lincoln has usually been treated as a gothic or a historical novel. Cooper intended it as the first in a series called "Legends of the Thirteen Republics." But perhaps he aborted the series because he realized he had produced in Lionel Lincoln something very different from a historical novel. For a discussion of the problem of genre in the novel, see Donald Ringe, "Cooper's Lionel Lincoln."

7

The Search for the Father

The Last of the Mohicans (I)

> The American landscape has never been at one with the
> white man. Never. And white men have probably never
> felt so bitter anywhere, as here in America, where the very
> landscape, in its very beauty, seems a bit devilish and
> grinning, opposed to us.
>
> D. H. Lawrence, "Fenimore Cooper's
Leatherstocking Novels"

If it is true that the novel is a solution to a problem that exists
for the writer,[1] then *The Last of the Mohicans* is Cooper's most
complex and hard-won solution. For it forms a violent argument about reality and examines, dramatically, the validity of
two antipodal ways of responding to nature.

For a long time, readers have been aware of the novel's
strange doubling, an effect which has often been regarded as a
mere narrative peculiarity. Its significance has been enlarged
in recent years by Leslie Fiedler, who focuses on the pairing of
the women characters and understands it as Cooper's (and the
nineteenth century's) need to isolate sexuality from the female
identity by creating two separate figures, one sexless and the
other darkly passionate.[2] But the doubling of female characters in *The Last of the Mohicans* is not unique (it occurs promi-
nently in *The Deerslayer* and in lesser works such as *Mercedes of*

---

1. For the development of this idea, see Charles Du Bos, "On the Inner
Environment' in the Work of Flaubert," in *Madame Bovary*, p. 360.

2. *Love and Death*, pp. 205–09. On the doubling of dark and light, also see
Lawrence, *Studies in Classic American Literature*, p. 58.

Castile), nor are other types of doubling, such as the division between "good" and "bad" Indians, unusual. What is interesting about *The Last of the Mohicans* is the extent of the doubling, for this novel in effect doubles itself.

We have seen how Cooper's narrative journeys are typically directed toward an "objective," usually a human structure, which imparts significance to the motion of journeying. *The Last of the Mohicans* is unusual in that it describes two complete and distinct journeys, each with its own objective. And these two objectives define and establish the polar values of Cooper's imaginative world. The novel divides, pivots as it were, in the center on a geographic fulcrum, a still point which allows the temporal flow to stop and reverse its direction. At this point, the narrative starts over as Cooper initiates a whole new journey and, in a sense, a whole new novel. Whereas the first journey leads "forward" into the future toward civilization and the world of the father, the second journey pushes "backward" into the time and space of the primitive and the eternal feminine.[3] In this way, the structure of the double journey establishes the two primary "directions" of Cooper's thought and art.

The geography of the first journey is a full realization of the landscape of difficulty. As Cora and Alice Munro travel with their protectors from "the encampment of Webb" (50) to Fort

3. Donald Darnell also divides the narrative into two parts and argues, as I do in the following chapter, that Uncas is the true hero of the tale. "In the first half of the novel," he says, "the action is set in the white man's world," whereas the "hostile territory" of the second half of the book is "another world, the Indian world, which is also the mythic world" ("Uncas as Hero: The *Ubi Sunt* Formula in *The Last of the Mohicans*"). But Darnell provides little more than an outline of this pattern, and by failing to fill out the narrative structure of the book with the rich imagery that supports it, he makes it possible for Thomas Philbrick to refute his entire argument and to categorize it as one of the "Simpler analyses" ("Sounds of Discord," p. 26). My analysis will show that Darnell was correct in discovering two distinct worlds in the novel, although my definitions of those worlds differ substantially from his. Also see Fiedler, pp. 205, 208; David Howard, "James Fenimore Cooper's *Leatherstocking Tales*," pp. 48–54; and Ringe, *James Fenimore Cooper*, pp. 43–44, *The Pictorial Mode*, p. 46.

William Henry in search of their father, the landscape seems to resist their passage at every turn. The wilderness through which they pass is in a state of violent transition; no longer the possession of the Indian, it is being contested by the English and the French but is controlled by no one. The atmosphere is oppressively hot, and the dominant spatial qualities are those of obstacle and difficulty. The descriptive terms, "broken" and "interrupted," occur with great frequency.

Although the novel is set in the forest, this landscape contains few of the pastoral images that fill the space of a book like *The Deerslayer*. "Bleak and black hills" characterize a surface which the travelers find "painful" to negotiate. They must labor through terrain that is "ragged with rocks, and intersected with ravines" (176). Most telling are the water images. Here we find nothing like the pure and pacific Glimmerglass. Rather than a central, unifying water image, there are many diverse and scattered bodies of water. Cooper shows us isolated rivulets, springs, a pond, a waterfall, and a "rebellious stream" (69). Where the Glimmerglass offers clear moral instruction, these bodies of water are not so easily understood. Their " 'whole design . . . seems disconcerted' " (68), as Hawkeye says of the turbulent river that rushes over Glens Falls. The waterfall itself " 'was, in its time, as regular and as handsome a sheet of water as any along the Hudson,' " but it has become " 'rebellious' " (67) and now " 'falls by no rule at all' " (68). The Glimmerglass radiates feminine repose, but the "rebellious stream" (69) resembles " 'a headstrong man' " who has broken " 'loose from order' " (68). And while the Glimmerglass is limpid and pure, these bodies of water show signs of spoliation. The salt spring contains "healing waters," but at this moment in history it is lined with "bodies of the dead . . . [which] fester on the neighboring mount" (155). And a once beautiful pond has become " 'the bloody pond' " (170), discolored by the bodies of many French soldiers who perished in an ambush and were given the water as their grave. Even the cave beneath Glens Falls is " 'full of cracks' " and " 'sadly changed' " to the point that it has " 'neither shape nor consistency' " (67).

Shortly before they reach their "objective," Fort William Henry, the characters are offered a momentary respite from the difficulties and hazards of their journey. A mountaintop "a thousand feet in the air" affords them a view of the entire surrounding landscape. As they look first toward the north—the direction in which their second journey will take them—they see a "limpid and, as it appeared from that dizzy height, the narrow sheet of the 'holy lake,' indented with numberless bays, embellished by fantastic headlands, and dotted with countless islands." "At the distance of a few leagues," the narrator continues, "the bed of the waters became lost among mountains, or was wrapped in the masses of vapor that came slowly rolling along their bosom, before a light morning air."

Their elevation also permits them to look back toward the south and gain a different, more distant, perspective upon the course of their arduous journey: "To the south stretched the defile, or rather broken plain, so often mentioned." "For several miles in this direction," we are told, "the mountains appeared reluctant to yield their dominion, but within reach of the eye they diverged, and finally melted into the level and sandy lands, across which we have accompanied our adventurers in their double journey." From this great height, the obstacles and deformities of that broken landscape are not visible. The "bloody pond," for example, cannot be seen; it is identified only by a "single, solitary, snow-white cloud [which] floated above the valley, and marked the spot beneath which lay the silent pool" (177).

Regardless of where Cooper directs our vision, this distant view of nature mitigates the harsh realities of the landscape. The "extensive earthen ramparts . . . of William Henry" and the "tents and military engines of an encampment of ten thousand men," which occupy a significant portion of the panorama, become part of the larger "spectacle" (178). This is the magnificent "far view" of nature that Cooper so loved. The perspective of great height allows the narrator a position of literal and moral elevation from which he can, as Cooper wrote in one of his travel books, perceive the "general beauties" while ignoring the "disgusting details."[4]

But this novel never pauses for long on the "general beauties." The characters determine quickly that to reach the fort they must pass through the French lines, and to do this they descend with "much toil and pain" (180) into the arena of violent warfare below. There they find the "disgusting details" of the "near view" of the landscape (such details are always the work of man). They are fired upon from every side, and a miasmic fog enshrouds and confuses them to the point of complete disorientation. Ultimately, they are guided to the fort by the furrow of a cannonball that has "ploughed" a "road" (181) through the earth. The landscape that appeared so glorious from the mountaintop is found, upon a closer examination, to have been brutally violated by the engines of war.

Up to this point in the novel, Hawkeye has demonstrated a cold and unfailing efficiency. But now he begins to falter. As he approaches the center of civilized warfare, his usually acute perception and certain judgment fail him. His plan to fire at his enemies in the hope they will " 'give way, or . . . wait for reinforcements' " fails, and at one point, having "lost the direction" (182), he mistakenly leads the party away from, rather than toward, the protection of William Henry. Somehow, Cora and Alice manage to reach the fort safely, despite the fact that Duncan Heyward leaves them momentarily unprotected while he characteristically rushes off to lead his old company. Heyward, a soldier "little accustomed to the warfare of the woods" (250), has enthusiastically returned to the form of civilized warfare he understands. As the two women stand "trembling and bewildered by this unexpected desertion," they are gathered into the arms of "an officer of gigantic frame, whose locks were bleached with years and service" (183–84), Munro himself.

Leatherstocking's situation is not so favorable, however.

4. *Excursions in Italy*, p. 154. For a discussion of this passage, see chap. 11.

Lacking " 'his usual good fortune' " (191), he is captured before he reaches the safety of William Henry. The image of his
return to the fort is one of emasculation and humiliation: "The
countenance of Hawk-eye was haggard and careworn, and his
air dejected, as though he felt the deepest degradation at
having fallen into the power of his enemies. He was without his
favorite weapon, and his arms were even bound behind him
with thongs, made of the skin of a deer" (188). His "descent" is
complete, for at this point in the novel's development Hawkeye, Chingachgook, and Uncas virtually disappear from the
narrative. The two chapters that follow the reuniting of Alice
and Cora with their father focus on the manners and deliberations of the white, civilized characters. Correspondingly, many
of the scenes are set in the domestic, indoor space of the fort,
where our attention is directed to the polite negotiations between Munro and the gentlemanly Montcalm, and upon
Duncan Heyward's wooing of Alice.[5]

This is the moment at which the novel balances between its
"forward" thrust to Fort William Henry and its "backward"
journey into the world of the Indian. At this still point in the
novel's action, a truce holds the fighting in check while the
military leaders work out the terms of surrender, and nature
seems to answer this "temporary suspension" (187) of hostilities:

> The evening was delightfully calm, and the light air from
> the limpid water fresh and soothing. It seemed as if, with
> the termination to the roar of artillery and the plunging of
> shot, nature had also seized the moment to assume her
> mildest and most captivating form. The sun poured down
> his parting glory on the scene, without the oppression of
> those fierce rays that belong to the climate and the season.
> The mountains looked green, and fresh, and lovely; tem-
> pered with the milder light, or softened in shadow, as thin
> vapors floated between them and the sun. The numerous
> islands rested on the bosom of the Horican, some low and

5. Cf. Darnell, p. 261.

sunken, as if imbedded in the waters, and others appearing to hover above the element, in little hillocks of green
velvet; among which the fishermen of the beleaguering
army peacefully rowed their skiffs, or floated at rest on the
glassy mirror, in quiet pursuit of their employment.

The scene was at once animated and still. All that per-
tained to nature was sweet, or simply grand; while those
parts which depended on the temper and movements of
man were lively and playful.

Two little spotless flags were abroad, the one on a salient
angle of the fort, and the other on the advanced battery of
the besiegers; emblems of the truce which existed, not
only to the acts, but it would seem, also, to the enmity of the
combatants. [187]

The moment is of course fragile and illusory; it is out of this
beautiful lake that Montcalm will watch Magua's "dark form
rise . . . and steal without further noise to the land" (213)
where the Indian will spark the bloody massacre. And in this
portion of the novel there are ominous references to the restlessness of the Mingoes. Nevertheless, a genuine quality of
stasis is achieved at this point because the reader knows that a
significant journey has reached its conclusion.

The painstaking search for the father has ended, and
Cooper uses the narrative hesitation to present the world of
Munro, the unmistakable father-figure of *The Last of the Mohicans*. Munro is of course the literal father of Alice and Cora and
thinks of himself as the father of the hundreds of men, women,
and children who inhabit Fort Henry. As he acknowledges,
" 'All that you see here, claim alike to be my children' " (217).
But in a fuller sense than that of military responsibility, he
represents those values associated in Cooper's imagination
with the father/maker of civilizations. As the commander of
the fort, he stands at the forward thrust of the European
conquest of the American wilderness and is the necessary
predecessor of Judge Marmaduke Temple. And the same
ambivalent treatment of the father that we saw in *The Pioneers*

can be found in Cooper's characterization of Munro. On the one hand, the Colonel is described as a figure of "military grandeur" (184) and of unimpeachable courage and honor, fully deserving the devotion that all his children, filial and adopted, have for him. Yet on the other, he is revealed to be seriously lacking in judgment and to be ultimately incapable of protecting those whom he is charged to protect. We are given to understand that both the credulity of Munro and the inattention (betrayal is hinted) of Montcalm—that other "father" of white civilization—are responsible for the hideous massacre that follows.

Earlier in the novel, Heyward (who can be seen as a younger version of Munro, subject to the same misconceptions about the wilderness) seemed to abandon Alice and Cora in a moment of danger. Now, in the massacre scene, Munro also commits an act of "desertion":

> "Father—father—we are here!" shrieked Alice as he [Munro] passed, at no great distance, without appearing to heed them. "Come to us, father, or we die!"
>
> The cry was repeated, and in terms and tones that might have melted a heart of stone, but it was unanswered. Once, indeed, the old man appeared to catch the sounds, for he paused and listened; but Alice had dropped senseless on the earth, and Cora had sunk at her side, hovering in untiring tenderness over her lifeless form. Munro shook his head in disappointment and proceeded, bent on the high duty of his station. [223–24]

Munro is granted the same excuse as Heyward was earlier, the call of a higher duty, yet it does not convince; the image of desertion remains with us, and that is Cooper's (perhaps unconscious) intention.

With "more than half the guns . . . bursted" and the "walls . . . crumbling" (192), Fort William Henry was in a state of collapse before the Indian attack. But the massacre completely destroys Munro's world. Hundreds of his "children" are slaughtered; his daughters are abducted by the sinister Magua, and the fort, that symbol of the structuring principles of an emerging civilization, is a "smouldering ruin" (229). The advance into the wilderness led by the "father" is now seen to have been premature. This harsh landscape and its savage inhabitants will not yet yield to the white man, and the force of this truth reduces Munro to a state of moronic helplessness from which he does not fully recover in the novel.

Munro's demise is important from several points of view. The true adventure quest of *The Last of the Mohicans* is enacted in the second half of the narrative, and in order for it to begin the father must be displaced. In a discussion of the works of Robert Louis Stevenson, Robert Kiely says that adventures "are possible only when the limiting authority symbolized by the male parent is absent." "A mother may be overridden, convinced, left temporarily behind. But the father must give way altogether."[6] The logic of this imperative applies to *The Last of the Mohicans*, which is, considered from one point of view, Cooper's finest tale of adventure.

In another sense too the destruction of Munro's world is "necessary." The landscape of the novel objectifies a state of being that is too full of contradiction to remain in its present condition. The primitive has been repressed by an unnatural order imposed by an intruding white culture. Lines of natural demarcation and distinction have been obscured, and the rhythms of Indian life have been broken. As Hawkeye tells Heyward, " '. . . the evil has been mainly done by men with white skins' " (287); he is referring to the introduction of alcohol and the corrupting influence of "avaricious traders" (359). It is " 'white cunning [that] has managed to throw the tribes into great confusion, as respects friends and enemies,' " thus " 'throwing everything into disorder' " (249). Old alliances are broken and, not less significantly, ancient enmities are suppressed: " 'it has ended in turning the tomahawk of brother against brother, and brought the Mingo and the Delaware to travel in the same path' " (287).

6. *Robert Louis Stevenson and the Fiction of Adventure*, p. 72.

As Cooper describes it, the neutral ground of *The Last of the Mohicans* has become intolerable. It conforms to Northrop Frye's category of "demonic" (as opposed to "apocalyptic"): "the world of the nightmare and the scapegoat, of bondage and pain and confusion; the world as it is before the human imagination begins to work on it and before any image of human desire, such as the city or the garden, has been solidly established; the world also of perverted or wasted work, ruins and catacombs, instruments of torture and monuments of folly." [7] Given such conditions, either the primitive must be driven out altogether (as happens in *The Pioneers*) so that a true civilization may become "solidly established," or civilization itself must be turned back. In this novel, Cooper chooses the latter "solution," writing with the sure knowledge that if the primitive is to reassert its power, the modern will have to be utterly and violently repudiated.

This accounts for the incredibly bloody nature of the massacre, for this event is the culmination of all the motions of journeying through the territory of the neutral ground. The massacre scenes of mass death and desolation were prefigured by "the dull and dreary water" (170) of the "bloody pond," and now the raging waters of the "rebellious stream" (69) can be seen as preparatory for the following description of the "angry" Horican, just after the massacre has taken place: "The crowded mirror of the Horican was gone; and, in its place, the green and angry waters lashed the shores, as if indignantly casting back its impurities to the polluted strand" (229). Our previous idyllic view of the Horican was but a glimpse into the distant future, a time when fishermen would float lazily upon the mountain lake on peaceful afternoons and when, as Cooper projects earlier in the novel, the "salt spring" would become one of the most popular watering places in a settled, pastoral America.

But at this moment in history the landscape that for a moment "had been found so lovely" (229) reverts to its "harshest

7. *Anatomy of Criticism*, p. 147.

but truest colors" (230). The world over which Munro had ruled is destroyed, and the land he and Montcalm had attempted to control is seen to return to a state of "wildness and desolation; and it appeared as if all who had profanely entered it had been stricken, at a blow, by the relentless arm of death" (230). The massacre that brings about this state of desolation is a bursting forth of the primal forces of the natural world, an act which has the effect of clearing the neutral ground of its "impurities."

With Munro's world devastated, leadership changes hands. Heyward's command to begin an immediate pursuit of Magua and his captives carries no authority now. Leatherstocking is in a position to insist that the deliberateness of the Indian be adopted and all activity wait until the next day. When the small party arises from the ashes of the fort on the following morning a new journey begins, one which leads to a region beyond the landscape of difficulty.[8]

8. In the original (1826) edition, the massacre scene concluded the novel's first volume. There is no doubt that the requirements of a two-volume format influenced Cooper's narrative structure in this and other works. But here we have a case in which such publishing requirements were in perfect correspondence with the spirit and movement of a book. For Cooper's knowledge of the massacre as a historical event, see David P. French, "James Fenimore Cooper and Fort William Henry," and Thomas Philbrick, "The Sources of Cooper's Knowledge of Fort William Henry."

8

Beyond the Landscape of Difficulty

The Last of the Mohicans (II)

> Lie to us,—dance us back the
> tribal morn!

Hart Crane, "The Dance"

Joseph Campbell writes of the beginning stages of the mythic quest: "The adventure is always and everywhere a passage beyond the veil of the known into the unknown; the powers that watch at the boundary are dangerous; to deal with them is risky; yet for anyone with competence and courage the danger fades." [1] In *The Last of the Mohicans*, the "boundary" is formed by the Horican; this body of water divides the old world of Fort William Henry from the new world of the second journey. Our travelers must cross the lake, where they are engaged by a party of fierce Hurons in canoes who block their entrance to the region of the unknown. As Hawkeye, Chingachgook, and Uncas successfully repel these sentinels, Heyward expresses his fears: " 'With foes in front, and foes in our rear, our journey is like to be one of danger.' " The scout's reply communicates exactly the sense of confidence that Campbell says is appropriate to the undertaking of the quest: " 'Danger! . . . no, not absolutely of danger; for with vigilant ears and quick eyes, we can manage to keep a few hours ahead of the knaves; or, if we must try the rifle, there are three of us who understand its gifts as well as any you can name on the borders' " (257).

---

1. *The Hero with a Thousand Faces,* p. 82.

Having beaten off the "powers that watch at the boundary," the travelers land on the western shore of the Horican and enter the region of the unknown:

> The party had landed on the border of a region that is, even to this day, less known to the inhabitants of the states, than the deserts of Arabia, or the steppes of Tartary. It was the sterile and rugged district which separates the tributaries of Champlain from those of the Hudson, the Mohawk, and the St. Lawrence. Since the period of our tale, the active spirit of the country has surrounded it with a belt of rich and thriving settlements, though none but the hunter or the savage is ever known, even now, to penetrate its wild recesses. [269]

Though this terrain is even more difficult than the landscape of the first journey, its difficulties are not those of the neutral ground. Rather, they are associated with the mythic quest. As Mircea Eliade says, the "road leading to the center is a 'difficult road,' " a "road [that] is arduous, fraught with perils because it is, in fact, a rite of the passage from the profane to the sacred." [2]

The novel's first journey—from the encampment of Webb to Fort William Henry—intersects two points on the space of a map. This is the kind of space that Edward T. Hall, in *The Silent Language*, calls a "co-ordinate system," space which "one gets into . . . by intersecting it with lines" (203). The characters in the novel "cross" this map-space, moving progressively between "the different points that commanded the facilities of the route" (13). But in the region of the second journey it is necessary to "penetrate," to "plunge into its depths" (269). Leatherstocking and his party have only the most general knowledge of where their journey will lead them; they know only, as Uncas puts it, that " 'the dark-hair [Cora] has gone towards the frost [north]' " (271). The narrator mentions in passing that Hawkeye, Chingachgook, and Uncas have probed parts of the area before, but at no point during the second

2. *The Myth of the Eternal Return*, p. 18.

journey do they show signs of recognition of the landscape; therefore, the effect is one of a totally unknown territory. This is a geography that cannot be intersected with lines. Even to this day, Cooper tells us, it is virtually unknown and unplotted[3]—suggesting a region (of the mind) which lies forever beyond the impact of the straight line. Neither the military formations of white warfare nor Templeton's grid can be imposed here. The natural formations of the wilderness are preserved in this undiscovered country, a region which excludes the " 'settlements' " that cause " 'hunting and war [to] . . . lose their beauty' " (267).

While the first journey is a search for the father and a testing of the values he represents, the second is defined by its "great and engrossing object—the recovery of the sisters" (284). At one level, this means simply that a "father [is] in quest of his children" (231), but the reversal has a far more profound significance. The true object of this journey is the eternal feminine, and its motions describe what Joseph L. Henderson, in his study of initiation patterns, calls the "return to the Mother" that follows from "the need for rebirth from the father."[4]

This new object, which can only be found in the mythic space of the Indian world, necessitates a different quality of movement through the wilderness. The landscape of the first journey contains landmarks (the deserted blockhouse, the "bloody pond," and the underground waterfall hideout—all of which remind Hawkeye of earlier campaigns), landmarks which make it possible to move through space by fixing on known points, the intersection of which forms a "route." But in the region of the second journey such abstract reckoning is impossible. Here the party must follow a trail, and in Cooper this means total dependence on immediate perception. As Leath-

3. Cooper had traveled parts of the first journey himself on a walking tour in 1824, but the area of the second journey was unknown to him at the time he wrote the novel. See Edward Everett Hale, Jr., "American Scenery in Cooper's Novels," p. 326.

4. *Thresholds of Initiation*, p. 81.

erstocking instructs the others in the art of pathfinding, he urges deliberateness and sensitivity: " 'Softly, softly, . . . we now know our work, but the beauty of the trail must not be deformed' " (235). A delicacy associated with the feminine object of the journey is required: " 'Touch the leaves lightly, or you'll disconsart the formation. That! that is the print of a foot . . . [of] the dark-hair's [Cora]' " (237).[5] In their pursuit of the sisters, these pathfinders must "read" nature. Rather than simply move through the landscape, they must move within it, follow its streams, inspect its grass and trees, and interpret all its signs sensitively and painstakingly: "He [Hawkeye] often stopped to examine the trees; nor did he cross a rivulet, without attentively considering the quantity, the velocity, and the color of its waters" (269–70).

Most white men are totally unequipped to perform this kind of activity, for, as Harold Rosenberg says in his parable of Braddock's defeat, the British soldiers do "not *see* the American trees."[6] Munro has already been rendered incompetent and Heyward has become virtually functionless. Shortly after the massacre, in the initial stages of the pursuit of Magua and the sisters, Duncan asks Leatherstocking what he can do to further the party's progress; he receives a brutal rebuff: " 'You! . . . yes, you can keep in our rear, and be careful not to cross the trail' " (239). The " 'white man's courage' " (263) of Heyward is ill suited to the wilderness experience, as are the rules of white man's warfare. As Hawkeye asks, concerning a hostile Indian's misdirected shot, " 'Do you think the bullet of that varlet's rifle would have turned aside, though his sacred Majesty the King had stood in its path?' " (256–57).

Eventually, the interpretation of the trail becomes too difficult even for Leatherstocking, and at this point only Uncas is able to "read a language that would prove too much for the

5. This statement and the one cited immediately before it are both made by Leatherstocking before the party crosses the Horican and enters the unknown region. But even at this point, in the initial attempts to find the trail of the two sisters, the essential motion of the second journey has been established.

6. *The Tradition of the New,* p. 14.

wisest of [white men]" (249).[7] Twice when the trail appears
hopelessly lost, Uncas finds the crucial print. This is a signal of
his emergence as the hero of the second journey and as the
realization of ancient Delaware prophecy. During the first
journey, his role is important but secondary, although his fight
with Magua is a prefiguring of the epic battle between them
that climaxes the novel's action. (In several respects the first
journey anticipates the second. In an early scene, for example,
Hawkeye, Chingachgook, and Uncas discuss the dispossession
of the Delawares and refer to Uncas as the last of the Mohicans.) Even during the initial stages of the second journey
Uncas is overeager, and Hawkeye finds it necessary more than
once to criticize and instruct him. But from this point onward,
his stature rises steadily.

Uncas's second "discovery [of a footprint]" (275) is crucial. It
makes it possible for Hawkeye to say confidently, " 'I can now
read the whole of it' " (274). The trail becomes "fresh and
obvious," and with progress "no longer delayed by uncertainty" (276), the movement of the journey accelerates. This
too distinguishes the second journey from the first. At no point
between Webb and William Henry did the travelers experience
steady movement toward their objective. Up to the very entrance of the fort, sudden interruptions break the flow of
motion. During the second journey, however, painstaking but

      7. Cooper's interest in the Indians' remarkable ability to "read" geography
may have been stimulated by John Heckewelder's account of the Lenni
Lenape: "The geographical knowledge of the Indians is really astonishing. I
do not mean the knowledge of maps, for they have nothing of the kind to aid
them; but their practical acquaintance with the country that they inhabit."
Heckewelder says that the Indians "can steer directly through the woods in
cloudy weather as well as in sunshine to the place they wish to go, at the distance
of two hundred miles and more. When the white people express their as-
tonishment, or enquire how they can hit a distant point with so much ease and
exactness, they smile and answer: 'How can we go wrong when we know where
we are to go?' " (*History, Manners, and Customs of the Indian Nations*, pp. 307–08).
Cf. *LM*, p. 44. See Roy Harvey Pearce for a brief summary of the probable
sources of and scholarship relating to Cooper's Indian lore (*Savagism and
Civilization*, pp. 200–01).

steady movement through space becomes rapid and sure progress toward the "center." Hawkeye shows his awareness of the significance of a crucial moment when he says, " 'our march is come to a quick end, and . . . we are in an enemy's country' " (272).

In their final thrust into the " 'enemy's country,' " the journeyers follow the course of a rill (274), an element of landscape contrasting strongly with the furrow of a cannonball which earlier guides them to Fort William Henry. As we enter a world of magic and myth, "the stream . . . expanded into a little lake, covering most of the low land, from mountain to mountain. The water fell out of this wide basin in a cataract so regular and gentle, that it appeared rather to be the work of human hands, than fashioned by nature" (277).

The placement and imagery of this scene are of critical importance, for the lake is the most intensely valued element in Cooper's imaginative geography. When it is experienced as a discovery, as it is here (and as it also is on the beginning pages of *The Deerslayer*), it always signals a return to the pristine world of nature. (We recall that in his travel journals, Cooper expresses the greatest delight over scenes which come upon him by surprise.) The lake's circular design suggests cohesion, and the stillness of its waters tells us that we have left the broken landscape of the neutral ground and have entered a region of purity. This small and placid lake should be seen in contrast to the bloody pond of the first journey, a body of water conforming to Northrop Frye's category of the demonic, in which "the world of water is the water of death, often identified with spilled blood." We move now from the demonic into the realm of the apocalyptic, the region of desire.[8]

The "cataract so regular and gentle" that spills out of the lake is strikingly different from the violent and "rebellious" Glens Falls of the first journey. This cataract appears to be "the work of human hands," a characteristic which identifies it with the valued images of park and garden that fill the narrative space

8. *Anatomy of Criticism,* p. 150.

of *The Oak Openings*. That the lake and waterfall have been created by beavers (it is not, as Heyward mistakenly thinks, inhabited by men) gives it even greater value, for we recall that the beaver pond Captain Willoughby finds in the virgin forest of New York State immeasurably enhances his discovery. Here, as in *Wyandotté*, the beavers are associated with the purity and timeless past of the natural world.[9] They have existed in this same area of the novel's geography "for hundreds of years" (415) and their presence measures the destructive changes recent history has brought to the surrounding territories. While white traders regard the animals in crude economic terms, the Indian, we are told, continues to "venerate the beaver" (325).

Cooper may have learned from John Heckewelder's account of the manners and myths of the Lenni Lenape that the "Indians consider the earth as their universal mother. They believe that they were created within its bosom, where for a long time they had their abode, before they came to live on its surface." The Delawares, Heckewelder explains, believed "that in the beginning, they dwelt in the earth under a lake." One of the members of the tribe is said to have discovered an opening and "ascended to the surface; on which, as he was walking, he found a deer, which he carried back with him into his subterranean habitation; that there the deer was killed, and he and his companions found the meat so good, that they unanimously determined to . . . remove to a place where they could enjoy the light of heaven and have such excellent game in abundance."[10] Thus, along with all its other associations, the lake symbolizes the origins of life (the Mother) and the passage to the plenitude of the natural world.

9. Although both *Wyandotté* and *The Oak Openings* were written much later than *Mohicans*, I am speaking here of a deep imaginative proclivity toward certain images which finds expression in the whole body of Cooper's fiction. As J. Hillis Miller says of Thomas Hardy, the writer's career may show change and development, but "the deeper configurations . . . remain the same from the beginning to the end" (*Thomas Hardy*, p. ix).

10. *History, Manners, and Customs*, pp. 249–50. Cf. Richard Slotkin's application of this myth to *The Pioneers*, in *Regeneration through Violence*, pp. 490–94.

The narrator of *The Last of the Mohicans* explains that the beaver pond creates and lies within a clearing, one of Cooper's most valued configurations, and that the journeyers first see it in "the glow of a mild summer's evening" (277). Except for the two broad panoramas we witnessed at the site of Fort William Henry (both deceptive because they hide the "disgusting details" that lie within them), this novel has been almost devoid of such pastoral imagery. But as we enter the timeless world of nature, these images begin to proliferate. We return to a world in which "the woods were again as still and quiet as a mild summer morning and deep solitude could render them" (407) and where "long and shadowed vistas of trees" (412) stretch into the distance. The forest, which in the first journey was drawn in images of difficulty, can now be seen to "spread itself like a verdant carpet of bright green against the side of the mountain" (405).

The novel's first journey—to Fort William Henry—is traveled in the stifling heat of late summer, and the massacre coincides with a "frightful change . . . in the season," a change which brings "the blasts of a premature November" (229). But as the image of "mild summer" indicates, the second journey has led us into a different climate; our return has come through time as well as space. To use Frye's categories, we have moved "backward" from the Mythos of Autumn (tragedy) to the Mythos of Summer (romance-adventure).[11]

In this region of romance, magical transformations begin to take place. These transformations are, as some have suggested, reminiscent of Shakespearean romance,[12] and Heyward's disguise is particularly theatrical. Yet the other disguises are far more suggestive of the metamorphoses of the mythic quest. There is no wide agreement on the function of "shape-shifting,"[13] a phenomenon very common to quest patterns, yet it is safe to say that in *The Last of the Mohicans* such transformations create the pervasive effect of union with the natural world. Even the effete David Gamut becomes an Indian. Chin-

11. *Anatomy of Criticism*, pp. 186–223.
12. For example, see Fiedler, p. 201.
13. See Lord Raglan, *The Hero*, pp. 258–64.

gachgook takes the form of a beaver, and Hawkeye becomes a
bear. Cooper must have been impressed by Heckewelder's
account of the Indian sense of oneness with nature and animals: "All animated nature, in whatever degree, is in their eyes
a great whole, from which they have not yet ventured to separate themselves. They do not exclude other animals from their
world of spirits, the place to which they expect to go after
death."[14]

In his quest toward the mythic center, Uncas must pass
through the "underworld," symbolized by the Huron village.
His courage is given its most extreme test in this "unhallowed
and supernatural arena, in which malicious demons had as-
sembled to act their bloody and lawless rites" (301). With "dark
glancing spectres" (292) on its outskirts, this arena provides the
setting for Uncas's rite of passage. Adjacent to the village and
part of its world is a cave—a literal under-world—through
which Uncas will later pass in his pursuit of the demonic
Magua. The cave "appeared like the shades of the infernal
regions, across which unhappy ghosts and savage demons were
flitting in multitudes" (424);[15] its identification with the Indian
spirit-world contrasts it markedly with the underground hideout at Glens Falls, a cave "sadly changed"—made profane—by
the erosion of history. The testing that Uncas undergoes in the
Huron village conclusively proves his bravery and worthiness,
and upon his release from the underworld he advances to the
sacred center.

It is highly significant that at this point in the novel Cooper

14. *History, Manners, and Customs*, p. 254.
15. This quotation serves well as an example of the way in which Cooper
mythicizes the action of the novel. The cave is not literally the underworld but
"appeared like" the underworld. Similarly, the "dark glancing spectres" that
seem to guard the village, we discover, are Indian children playing in the grass.
Because *The Last of the Mohicans* is a novel, it cannot enact "pure" or "undis-
placed" myth. Instead, the repeated use of certain similes begins to create a
mythical effect. This corresponds with what Frye calls "the general tendency
we have called romantic, the tendency to suggest implicit mythical patterns in a
world more closely associated with human experience" (pp. 139–40).

for the first time separates the two sisters. The pale and faint-
ing Alice remains with the Hurons while Cora is placed in the
Delaware camp. During the first journey, Uncas shows a special interest in Cora and his interest is returned in the "dark
hair's" barely concealed fascination with the beautiful Indian
warrior. Cora's rich coloring (derived from a remote Negro
ancestress) and her sensuous beauty identify her strongly with
the Indian world and with nature.[16] Like Judith Hutter in *The
Deerslayer*, her beauty merges with and heightens the beauty of
the landscape: "the colors of her dress were blended with the
foliage of the forest" (402). Cooper's placement of Cora (without Alice) at the "center," the Delaware camp, confirms her
identity as the feminine object of the mythic quest.

As Cooper describes the Delaware camp, he draws our attention to "a large and silent lodge in the centre of the village"
(362), a mysterious structure that is the symbolic center of *The
Last of the Mohicans*. This is the "sacred lodge" which Eliade says
is always positioned "in the middle of the village"; it represents
"the Center of the World," the axial point from which the
"universe comes to birth."[17] Tamenund's lodge is the point
toward which all the motions of the second journey have been
directed. As the center of the sacred space of the Indian world,
it stands in implicit contrast to the center of profane space, Fort
William Henry. And while the fort is the "house" of civilization's father, this "large and silent lodge" is the home of the
sage of the Indian world. More than a century old, Tamenund
possesses "the peculiar recollection of vast age" (385). He is the
living symbol of the natural past and "remembers"—contains
within him—a time before the white man had landed on
American shores. It is given to him to articulate fully the theme
of the eternal return and to recognize in Uncas the realization

16. My reading deemphasizes the importance of miscegenation, which Leslie Fiedler sees as the "secret theme" (205) of the novel. For other perspectives
on Cora's racial identity, see George Dekker, *James Fenimore Cooper the Novelist*,
p. 68; James Grossman, *James Fenimore Cooper*, p. 45; Joel Porte, *The Romance in
America*, p. 22; Nina Baym, "The Women of Cooper's Leatherstocking Tales,"
p. 705.

17. *The Sacred and the Profane*, pp. 44–46.

of that return, a moment prepared for by the entire second journey.

When Uncas, assumed to be an enemy of the tribe, is brought before Tamenund, the sage listens to the young warrior's "musical voice," and as he does so all remaining sounds of discord are muffled by the sounds of harmony: " 'Does Tamenund dream!' he [Tamenund] exclaimed. 'What voice is at his ear! Have the winters gone backward! Will summer come again to the children of the Lenape!' " This seemingly "incoherent burst" (389) is not understood by the other members of the tribe, and Uncas is prepared for torture by fire: "The circle broke its order, and screams of delight mingled with the bustle and tumult of the preparation." But the image of the tortoise on Uncas's chest reveals him to be the lost leader of the tribe, and as he advances "with the air of a King" (391), Tamenund recalls, almost repossesses, "the days of happiness" (392). The "days of happiness" refer to that time before a destructive European culture had caused "the violent separation of the vast tribes of the Delawares" (287). In describing the effects of this intrusion—an intrusion which introduced to the New World what Claude Lévi-Strauss calls "the agitations of " 'history' "[18]—Tamenund employs imagery which has become familiar to us: " 'I have lived to see the tribes of the Lenape driven from their council fires, and *scattered*, like *broken herds of deer*' " (389; my italics).[19] But with the "return" of Uncas, this image of interruption and dispersion is replaced by one of cohesion: "once more they [the Delaware warriors] stood ranged in their circle" (393). The closing of the circle symbolizes the restoration of the unity of the natural world.

The emergence of the lost leader of the tribe is so stunning an event that the ancient wise man wonders if time has not literally gone backward and asks, " 'Is Tamenund a boy?' " (392). His recognition of Uncas brings "a flash of recollection [which has the effect of] . . . restoring him at once to a con-

18. *Tristes Tropiques*, p. 78.
19. Cf. Cooper's treatment of "the last Sachem of the broken and dispersed tribe of the Narragansetts" (461) in *The Wept of Wish-ton-Wish*.

sciousness of the true history of his nation" (392). As we follow Tamenund's narration of this true history, we are reminded of Lévi-Strauss's account of a Brazilian tribe of " 'former savages' " who, "thrown back upon their own resources," experienced "a strange reversal of the apparent equilibrium between 'modern' and 'primitive' cultures. Old ways of life and traditional techniques reappeared; the 'past' to which they belonged was, after all, neither dead nor distant" (135).

The question put earlier by Tamenund, " 'Will summer come again to the children of the Lenape!' " is answered by nature, for the setting of Uncas's emergence is a "mild summer morning" (407). As we have seen, summer symbolizes the return, and morning suggests renewal. Now, as Cooper describes the scene of the anticipated battle between the Delawares and the Hurons, nature replies fully to the human events that have recently taken place in the Indian village. Nowhere, he tells us, "was any object to be seen that did not properly belong to the peaceful and slumbering scenery." Here is an image of a totally integrated landscape; it exhibits none of the broken terrain of the neutral ground. The narrator directs our vision toward a "verdant and undulating surface of forest, which spread itself *unbroken* [my italics], unless by stream or lake, over such a vast region of country." Cooper tells us that across "the tract of wilderness, which lay between the Delawares and the village of their enemies, it seemed as if the foot of man had never trodden, so breathing and deep was the silence in which it lay" (412).

The battle that follows is a return to the ancient, uncorrupted enmity between the tribes. Now that Delaware and Huron are no longer joined in an unnatural alliance, the full "harmony of warfare" (250) is restored. Although violent death results from the fighting, at no point do we experience it as carnage.[20] Rather, Cooper focuses our attention on the

20. Donald Ringe misreads, I think, when he finds it a "scene of bloody carnage" and misses the significance of the Indian fight when he says that it is not "sensible" (*The Pictorial Mode*, pp. 46–47). See Paul Goodman's distinction between natural violence and artificial violence in *The Empire City*.

animal-like grace of Indian combat: "Without stopping to breathe, the Delawares leaped, in long bounds, towards the wood, like so many panthers springing upon their prey" (419). The only European soldier to take part in the hostilities is Heyward, and his role is minor. Although he wishes aloud for his troops, telling Hawkeye that the " 'bayonet would make a road' " through the enemy's defenses, it is clear that the "straight line" of military formation has no place in this battle. Leatherstocking explains to him that natural warfare requires not bayonets but a " 'ready hand, a quick eye, and a good cover.' " While Hawkeye is in a position to instruct Heyward in " 'the philosophy of an Indian fight' " (418), he too assumes a lesser role than is customary for him, having relinquished the overall command to Uncas. And as if to confirm that this is an "Indian fight," he turns over his band of warriors to Chingachgook: "Hawk-eye . . . resigned the chief authority into the hands of the Mohican chief" (420).

At the close of the first journey, as the characters approach Fort William Henry, we are given a distant view of the battlefield from a position of great elevation. Now we witness a comparable panorama as Cooper describes the scene of the battle between the Hurons and the Delawares: "The land fell away rather precipitately in front, and beneath their eyes [the viewers are Hawkeye and his band] stretched, for several miles, a narrow, dark, and wooded vale. It was through this dense and dark forest that Uncas was still contending with the main body of the Hurons." But this visual survey of "the leafy bosom of the valley" reveals none of the "engines" of European warfare that take up so prominent a portion of the earlier rendered spectacle. Here the elements of the landscape are without exception pastoral, and even the smoke of weapons is immediately absorbed by the natural scene: "here and there a light vapory cloud, which seemed already blending with the atmosphere, arose above the trees, and indicated some spot where the struggle had been fierce and stationary" (421).

The climax of the battle and of the novel's action is the epic confrontation between Uncas and Magua. We have seen how

Uncas's stature has risen to mythic proportions during the course of the second journey, but this is also true of Magua. He is no longer the treacherous, secret ally of the French whose penchant for drink gives him away. Now he serves not the French but himself and his tribe. Like Rivenoak in *The Deerslayer*, this "bad Indian" speaks an eloquent denunciation (in the Delaware village) of the white man's "gluttony" (381) and thereby establishes a historical justification for his intense hatred. In the second half of the book, he also appears to regain the favor of his tribe and becomes its spokesman and, tacitly, its leader. Even his lustful pursuit of Cora has about it a quality of pure malignancy that lifts him to the level of the legendary foe. No longer the sly pawn of the French, he becomes "the Prince of Darkness" (359).[21] The metaphors that describe his actions in the battle scene suggest this legendary identification: "Still Magua, though daring and much exposed, escaped from every effort against his life, with that sort of fabled protection that was made to overlook the fortunes of favored heroes in the legends of ancient poetry" (423–24). This fabled protection has functional importance, for it preserves Magua for the final confrontation between himself and Uncas, a confrontation which takes on the significance of a struggle between pure Good and pure Evil.

In ancient myth, the hero often dies on a hilltop, a point from which he ascends to the sky. The conclusion of *The Last of the Mohicans* is suggestive of this pattern. A descent into a valley (the Valley of Death) leads toward the climax of the first journey. And the aftermath of the massacre is rendered in images of desolation and the putrefaction of corpses "blackened beneath the fierce heats of August": "hundreds of human forms . . . were stiffening in their deformity" (229). But the second journey climaxes after an ascent to the cool and pure atmosphere of a mountaintop; the moment is prepared for not by images of mass death and modern warfare but by the "harmony" of "an Indian fight." With the novel's stage so

21. Cf. Terence Martin, "From the Ruins of History," pp. 227–29.

perfectly set for epic combat, Cooper creates one of his most strikingly dramatic scenes, in which Magua kills the wounded Uncas and then plummets a thousand feet to his own death after having been shot by Hawkeye. The scene has all the (spatial) coherence and the (temporal) inevitability of the conclusion of the tragic epic. As we view the slain Uncas lying by the side of Cora, who is killed moments earlier by one of Magua's "assistants" (426), we experience a sense of an ending that the climax of the first journey does not give us. This ending, then, has also been a return. For the novel implicitly states that such epic action is no longer possible in the modern world—a world in which warfare is conducted by masses of indistinguishable soldiers and their destructive engines. Only the past, Cooper seems to say, can provide the context for true heroism.

The doubling of *The Last of the Mohicans* is far more extensive, functional and systematic than any of Cooper's critics have recognized. Traditionally, the novel has been considered one of his most well-made tales, but this praise has often brought with it the judgment that this " 'pure' adventure story is deliberately superficial." In James Grossman's words, "It has no serious concern with the outside world which it uses as a decoration and an aid to the action" (44). In part that misconception derives from Cooper himself, who instructed his readers that *The Last of the Mohicans* was simply a "narrative," stating that it had no "imaginary" or "romantic" significance.[22] But Cooper is an unreliable guide in such matters, and this is clearly a case in which we should follow Lawrence's instruction to trust the tale, not the teller.[23] Although *The Last of the Mohicans* is a well-made adventure, its design has a far more profound significance. As we have seen, the double journey lays out the polar regions of Cooper's imaginative geography, and the structure can be schematized in this way:

22. In the original (1826) preface, p. iii.
23. *Studies in Classic American Literature*, p. 2.

The First Journey	*The Second Journey*
The neutral ground (the landscape of difficulty)	The region of the mythic quest (the pastoral landscape)
Map-space	Primitive (mythic) space
Abstract reckoning	Immediacy of perception
The "line" and the "grid"	The circle
"Broken"	"Unbroken," whole
The present	The past
"Progress" (linear time)	The eternal return (cyclical time)
Spoliation	Purity
Discord	Harmony
White warfare (destructive)	Indian warfare (natural, harmonious)
Reality	Desire
Masculine	Feminine
Profane	Sacred

The individual images of the landscape conform to this system of polarities, and some of the more important pairings follow:

Glens Falls ("rebellious")	"a cataract so regular and gentle"
Underground waterfall hideout	The Huron cave
The "bloody pond"	The beaver pond
Cannon furrow as guide	Stream as guide
Fort William Henry	Tamenund's lodge
Panorama of civilized warfare	Panorama of Indian warfare
Massacre scene (descent)	Scene of epic combat (ascent)

Correspondingly, the characters are set in symbolic opposition:

Munro (father of civilization)	Tamenund (sage of the Indian world)
Heyward (civilization's hero)	Uncas (hero of the mythic quest)
Alice (civilization's "prize")	Cora (object of the mythic quest)
Magua as corrupted by the French	Magua as "the Prince of Darkness"

Several of the novel's main characters—Hawkeye, Chingachgook, and David Gamut—are not included in this schema because they do not include themselves. Each in his own way exists outside the lines of force established by the novel's polarities. Chingachgook's role in *The Last of the Mohicans* is less significant than in any of the other three Leatherstocking tales in which he appears. Largely, this is because his usual place as Hawkeye's heroic Indian companion has been taken by Uncas, who requires the largest possible stage on which to assert his mythic stature as the last of the Mohicans. For this reason, in the final section of the novel when Uncas assumes leadership of the Delawares, Chingachgook is relegated to the invisible function of protecting the senile Munro in the obscurity of a secret hiding place. Only in the final battle scene, when Leatherstocking turns over the command of his party to the chief, does Chingachgook finally assume "the station to which his birth and experience gave him so distinguished a claim" (420). In this novel, his role is necessarily that of proud father and observer of his son's rise to greatness.

David Gamut wanders in and out of the action, free to roam because the Indians pity what they consider to be his insanity. At one level, Cooper is contrasting the effete songster with the rugged Leatherstocking (Hawkeye never tires of ridiculing Gamut's ineffectuality). David, however, is not merely the foil for the scout's diatribes against gentility and "bookish knowledge." He provides a genuine perspective—a "literary" counterpoint—on the novel's action by interpreting the events as they happen in terms of biblical analogy. On one level, this is facetious and ironic,[24] yet on another it works to intensify the legendary quality of the narrative.

Of the three outsiders, Hawkeye's case is the most interesting and the most indicative of Cooper's real solution to the problem of the novel. This Natty Bumppo is different from the character we encounter in the other Leatherstocking tales. In

24. John J. McAleer emphasizes Cooper's ironic treatment of Gamut ("Biblical Analogy in the Leatherstocking Tales," pp. 223–25).

The Pioneers, he is an ineffectual old man who is finally forced to leave his beloved woods. In *The Prairie* Cooper makes him a sage and very nearly apotheosizes him. The last-written of the tales, *The Pathfinder* and *The Deerslayer,* present an infantile hero, a child of the forest. Unlike any of these works, *The Last of the Mohicans* characterizes a hardened, adult Leatherstocking. The "killer" whom Lawrence mistakenly saw in all of the tales is certainly present in this novel. Hawkeye is, as Lawrence calls him, an "isolate, almost selfless, stoic, enduring man, who lives by death, by killing, but who is pure white."[25] Here is a figure of "stern and unyielding morality" (*LM*, 93) who, like Kurtz, can unhesitatingly order the command, " 'Extarminate the varlets!' " (141) and who can unflinchingly drive "the sharp weapon through his [Indian enemy's] naked bosom to the heart" (88).

These examples of Hawkeye's killer instinct are taken from the part of the novel that enacts the journey from the encampment of Webb to Fort William Henry. On one level, they reflect the hard necessities imposed by the hazardous landscape of the neutral ground. In each of the Leatherstocking tales, Natty Bumppo's character corresponds to the novel's setting, and just as the hero of the idyllic world of *The Deerslayer* is almost Wordsworthian in his admiration of nature, the Leatherstocking of *The Last of the Mohicans* is as hard, cold, and efficient as the setting is arduous and difficult. The narrator assures us that, in the chaotic and unpredictable world of the first journey, deeds of "apparent cruelty . . . [are] of real necessity" (57).

We have seen how the entrance into the region of the mythic unknown awakens Uncas's sense of destiny, and we expect that Hawkeye, having emerged from his "degradation" into a world in which he has unquestioned authority, will also undergo a change. To some extent, our expectations are met. In the second half of the novel, Leatherstocking leaves behind some of the "cold indifference" (72) that characterizes him

25. *Studies in Classic American Literature,* pp. 59, 63.

during the first journey; his love for his Indian companions is
emphasized, and he becomes less the "killer," less the "stoic."
But strangely, he does not become less defensive. His attacks
on the inexperience of Heyward become more frequent and
more caustic as the journeyers move deeper into Indian territory. Duncan's misapprehension of the beaver colony brings
one of Hawkeye's characteristic taunts: " 'so much for school-
ing and passing a boyhood in the settlements' " (279). Indeed,
Leatherstocking literally makes a "fool" (289) of Heyward
when he instructs Chingachgook to disguise the young officer
in "the masquerade of a buffoon" (290). Even more difficult to
understand is the scout's almost brutal treatment of the harmless David Gamut. David's appearance in Indian garb causes
Hawkeye a "merriment . . . [that] was not easily appeased"
(281), but like the "unrestrained and heartfelt laughter" (279)
expressed earlier at Heyward's expense, this merriment is
defensive and self-protective. Leatherstocking is looking for
opportunities to laugh. Perhaps the most revealing of these
attacks comes when he fervently and cruelly declares that
" 'Kill-deer' [will never] become as harmless as the tooting
we'pon [Gamut's flute] of the singer' " (337). It is clear that
although Leatherstocking has entered a region in which his
leadership and prowess are virtually unchallenged he continues to feel the threat of emasculation and dispossession.

Why should this be? The answer is contained in a passage
which lies on the same page as the narrator's analogy between
Indian combat and the grace of the panther. At this point in
the battle, Leatherstocking pauses to reflect upon the
capacities of another animal, one which has been domesticated: " 'No—horse,' continued the scout [speaking to Hey-
ward], shaking his head, like one who mused; 'horse, I am
ashamed to say, must, sooner or later, decide these skrim-
mages. Put a shodden hoof on the moccasin of a red-skin; and
if his rifle be once emptied he will never stop to load it again' "
(418–19). Hawkeye perceives the eventual and certain extinction of "the harmony of warfare" and of the Indian himself.
Because the "American forest admits of the passage of horse,

there being little underbrush, and few tangled brakes" (418n.), the introduction of mounted troops into the landscape is inevitable. And with "horse" will come the settlements and, ultimately, dispossession. It is Hawkeye's refusal to deny the inevitability of these developments—the inevitability of history—which accounts for his continuing bitterness and which also distinguishes him from every other character in the novel.

All of the characters ranged on either side of the diagram above are blind to the truth of history. Both groups are so fully committed to the pursuit of their separate and polar destinies that they are utterly unconscious of the forces that can wreck their dreams. We have seen how Munro's premature "settlement" of the wilderness brings devastation. And nothing, not even the massacre, teaches the opaque and impatient Duncan Heyward that the methods of white warfare will not work in a truly primitive environment. But while Munro and Heyward are blind to history in that they have misjudged the historical moment, Hawkeye knows that their descendants will complete the white journey. It is simply a matter of "time." The greater misconception—the greater, but more beautiful, "lie"—is that cherished by Tamenund. He believes that because " 'the season of blossoms has always come again' " its ultimate return is inevitable. The past, he acknowledges, shows a history of dispossession, but as he attempts to pierce the future with his vision, he thinks he sees a time when the white man, who " 'entered the land at the rising . . . may yet go off at the setting sun' " (386). Even his sad remarks in the speech that closes the novel contain an implicit faith in the return: " 'The palefaces are masters of the earth, and the time of the red-men has not *yet* come again' " (443; my italics). His faith is in fact a refusal to enter history, a refusal to relinquish "mythical" for "concrete" time and to acknowledge what Eliade calls "the irreversibility of events."[26]

For Hawkeye, that denial is impossible. Although he would

26. *The Myth of the Eternal Return*, pp. 21–22, 74–75. Cf. *Black Elk Speaks*.

like to annul the effects of time, he knows that there can be no
real return. In the most important ways he stands outside the
two dramas, white and red, that structure the novel's action
and meaning. He passes through the two landscapes of *The Last
of the Mohicans* not as a hero, or a quester, but as the "guide"—
serving as both literal guide and as the mythological guide of
the quest. After leading Heyward to his proper center, Fort
Henry, he then prepares Uncas to seek his destiny in the
depths of Indian country. Nowhere is his distance better con-
veyed than in the crucial scene in which Uncas bounds up the
mountainside, followed by Heyward, in an attempt to save
Cora from Magua. Hawkeye lags behind, partly because his
rifle encumbers him but, more importantly, because he is "not
sustained by so deep an interest in the captive as his companions" (425).

At several points in the novel, there is a curious coincidence
between authorial commentary and Leatherstocking's observations. Just five pages before Natty expresses fierce resent-
ment of Montcalm, the narrator makes a severe historical
judgment upon the French commander. And the scout's
"strong expression of contempt" (286) for "the singer" seems
to be anticipated by the writer's sardonic reference to "David
Gamut, the master of psalmody" (281). As we read, we suspect
that Leatherstocking's bitterness is shared by his creator, and it
is interesting to note that *The Last of the Mohicans* is the only one
of the Leatherstocking tales in which Natty Bumppo is approximately the same age as Cooper was at the time the novel was
written. In the other four works, a relatively young author
portrays an old man (*The Pioneers, The Prairie*) or an older
writer romantically depicts the idyll of youth (*The Pathfinder,
The Deerslayer*). But this novel presents a forty-year-old Leatherstocking who is at the crisis of the midpoint. Like the difficult
landscape of the first journey, he is approaching the confusing
middle stage of development when youth (the pastoral) is gone
and powers have begun to fail. Unable to detect a "bauble" on
the ground (the young and vigorous Uncas finds it without
difficulty), Natty laments that it is " 'a certain sign of age, when

the sight begins to weaken' " (240). Because vision is the most important faculty possessed by Cooper's heroes, its failure threatens the loss of potency (Natty insists that he can " 'squint along . . . [the] clouded barrel [of Kill-deer] yet' ") and the diminishing of those vital capacities, such as pathfinding, that give Hawkeye his name(s) and establish his identity.

The popular conception of Cooper's development is that at the age of thirty he blithely began a prosperous authorship. The truth is very different. Although his first novels were extremely successful, a large portion of his substantial earnings was consumed in an attempt to keep the crumbling Cooper estate intact. Economic depression, his brothers' mismanagement, and a series of other misfortunes had, by 1820, brought the Cooper family to the point of financial ruin. The claims of creditors as well as the financial needs of the widows of four of the novelist's brothers (all four brothers died untimely deaths by 1819) put enormous pressures on Cooper in the early 1820s. There are indications that the Hudson River walking tour in the fall of 1824—the tour that inspired him to write *The Last of the Mohicans*—was intended to give relief from these pressures.[27] It may be that the constant threat of actual dispossession of the Cooper estate is reflected in Leatherstocking's unceasing bitterness and defensiveness. Further, Cooper seems to charge his rendering of the Indian's destruction with his fears of the destruction of his own world. We have observed in *The Pioneers* how the ancient claims of the Indian are linked in Cooper's imagination with the claims of the landed gentry.

While *The Pioneers* records a dispossession, however, its treatment of the theme is not direct. Rather, the writer maintains a wry and ironic distance between himself and his subject, as if to say, "It doesn't matter." But *The Last of the Mohicans*, more than any novel Cooper ever wrote, faces up to the reality of dispossession and to the terror of history. Some of Cooper's

27. See James F. Beard's commentary in *L&J*, 1:84; also see Beard's "Afterword" to *The Last of the Mohicans*, pp. 418–20.

critics have argued that this work is anything but a historical novel, pointing out that it pays only fleeting and perfunctory attention to the actual events of the French and Indian Wars.[28] But they have failed to recognize that although *The Last of the Mohicans* is not a period piece it takes account of the *force* of history more fully than any of Cooper's other works. In a profound sense, it is *about* history.

Donald Davie and others find the elegiac tone of the final scene unconvincing,[29] yet the effectiveness of the novel's conclusion needs to be reconsidered. The elegy enacted by the Indian maidens and pronounced by Munro is deliberately undercut by Cooper, who, through the perspective of Leatherstocking, implies a deeper tragedy than is felt by either the white or red mourners. (This deeper tragedy is also suggested by the French soldier, whose presence in the final scene is not very well explained by Cooper. On one level, he is introduced to show the temporary unity of the warring factions, but at another his presence confirms the intrusion of primitive space by the modern world.)

Joseph Campbell writes that the mythic quest is completed only when the hero brings "the runes of widsom, the Golden Fleece, or his sleeping princess, back into the kingdom of humanity, where the boon may redound to the renewing of the community, the nation, the planet, or the ten-thousand worlds." This full return signifies the joining of the two worlds, known and unknown, and it is the hero's task to show that "the two kingdoms are actually one" (193, 217). But, Campbell observes, stories and legends from all parts of the world are full of examples of heroes who fail, through death or other calamity, to make the return. *The Last of the Mohicans* is an example of such a "failure."

The Indian maidens sing of the heavenly marriage of Uncas and Cora—a marriage which suggests the joining of the two worlds of the novel. Even Munro, in his moment of greatest sorrow, speaks of the union of Indian and white and looks

28. For example, see Grossman, pp. 43–48.
29. *The Heyday of Sir Walter Scott,* p. 111.

ahead to a time " 'without distinction of sex, or rank, or color' "
(439). But to both the song of the Indian maidens and to
Munro's prediction, Leatherstocking shakes his head in doubt.
It is true that Hawkeye has rather fixed notions about racial
distinctions (he announces several times in the novel that he is
"a man without a cross"), but his gesture has a deeper meaning,
for it signifies his awareness that history has made such a union
impossible. Only at the very beginning of the white man's
exploration of America, and perhaps not even then, could
such a marriage have taken place. Now, the civilizing process
must work itself inexorably through the destructive stages of
possession and settlement until, hopefully, a true civilization is
formed. But the cost of this process, Hawkeye and the narrator
know, is the destruction of the Indian world, a world which has
been lost. For Cooper had already written the novel in which
Chingachgook, who is truly the *last* of the Mohicans, disappears from the land.

Leatherstocking's solution to the problem of dispossession is
a stoic affirmation of brotherhood with Chingachgook: " 'Sa-
gamore, you are not alone' " (442). Cooper's solution is the
novel itself. The writing of *The Last of the Mohicans* is the most
significant act in his development as a novelist. For it
dramatizes a symbolic exploration into a "past of legends," a
past which Bachelard says "opens a thousand paths to reverie."
The Last of the Mohicans does not complete the journey; it can
more properly be thought of as a "motion toward." But it
located for Cooper the place in which to seek and build a world
protected from the ravages of history, a world which, as
Bachelard writes, does not "run along the thread of a history."[30] Ironically, perhaps, this place of the imagination is
most fully defined by the novel's villain, Magua, in his denunciation of white "gluttony": " '[The Great Spirit] gave them [the
Indians] this island as he had made it, covered with trees, and
filled with game. The wind made their clearings; the sun and
rains ripened their fruits; and the snows came to tell them to be

30. *The Poetics of Reverie*, pp. 156, 192.

thankful. What need had they of roads to journey by! They saw through the hills!' " (381). This is the "island" of pastoral space Cooper would describe most fully and beautifully in *The Deerslayer*, a novelistic world far from the "roads" of the settlement and dominated by the spirit of the child rather than by that of the father.

After the writing of *The Last of the Mohicans*, the landscape of difficulty would never again occupy such a large part of Cooper's imaginative geography as it had in the early 1820s. The two works that follow it convey the sense of a sudden release from the ambiguous and uncertain terrain of the neutral ground. Both *The Prairie* and *The Red Rover* depict settings of unmitigated vastness. Each is a celebration of the terrible sublime, a region of absolute moral and spatial freedom.

At the same time that *The Last of the Mohicans* releases Cooper from the landscape of difficulty, it also announces the most significant journey of his own life, his trip to Europe. Since at least 1823, he had been restless to leave America and travel abroad, and shortly after publication of *The Last of the Mohicans*[31] he and his family made final preparations. On June 1, 1826, he embarked upon the most important voyage of his career, a voyage which would change everything. Europe became for him (perhaps it already was, before he left America) the source of the true civilized pastoral. It was the measure by which he would gauge his country's progress beyond its early, unsettled, and "raw" state of being.

After *The Last of the Mohicans*, Cooper did not return to the fictional setting of the American forest until *The Wept of Wish-ton-Wish*, written entirely in Europe and published in 1829. This novel's highly formal and centralized setting, as well as its pastoral descriptions of the interior forest, show that Cooper had absorbed a landscape of order and civilized beauty. And all of the forest novels he would write upon his return to America

31. *The Last of the Mohicans* was published by Carey and Lea on February 6, 1826 (source: Robert E. Spiller and Philip C. Blackburn, *A Descriptive Bibliography*, p. 43).

would evidence his altered conception of the wilderness. As Lawrence recognized, Cooper's deepest wish was to mitigate the "resistance" of nature: "He *wants* the landscape to be at one with him. So he goes away to Europe and sees it as such. It is a sort of vision."[32] By going abroad, Cooper literally left behind the landscape of difficulty that America had become for him. But Europe itself could never be the real destination. His destination was an America which he would transform, through art, to conform with his pastoral vision.

32. *Studies in Classic American Literature,* p. 56.

PART IV

The Aesthetics of Permanence

It is true that the provinces a little further south, such as
New Jersey, Pennsylvania, Maryland and Virginia, think
they can beat us in peaches; but I have never tasted any
fruit that I thought would compare with that of Satanstoe.
I love every tree, wall, knoll, swell, meadow and hummock
about the old place.

Satanstoe

9

Protecting the Island

> The distinction between self and not-self is made by the
> childish decision to claim all that the ego likes as "mine,"
> and to repudiate all that the ego dislikes as "not-mine." It
> is as simple as that.
>
> Norman O. Brown, Love's Body

Critics have treated the matter of "boundary" in Cooper's
fiction almost exclusively in terms of the writer's political
attitudes, and in relation to his identity as a member of a
threatened gentry. But as Norman O. Brown writes, the sense
of boundary originates at a deeper level.[1] There is no doubt
that much of Cooper's concern about the unstable middle layer
of society derives from his political experience and values. Yet
there is something more. Scattered throughout the letters is
evidence that his deep sense of threat to his personal space and
possessions was at least as much a function of personality as it
was a function of ideology.

Consider, for example, an extended correspondence
Cooper had with the Department of the Navy shortly after he
resigned his commission. The correspondence deals with a
small cash debt which the navy claimed Cooper had incurred
while in the service. Cooper insisted, in a series of letters, that
he owed the navy nothing and in fact had suffered losses.[2]
What is interesting about these letters is not that Cooper
should have insisted upon his rights but that the tone is so

---

1. See Brown's chapter entitled "Boundary," from which the headnote to
this chapter is taken (*Love's Body*, pp. 141–61).
2. See esp. the letters numbered 53, 56, 61, and 63 in *L&J*, vol. 1.

recognizable. Here there is no issue of property in an abstract sense, only a matter of $190.79. Yet the tone of these letters, written when Cooper was a very young man, is the same insistent and strident tone that the much older author of *The Redskins* employs in a defense of property rights. Repeatedly the narrator of the novel uses the words "my" and "mine," and sometimes they are even italicized as in the following passage: "I drove our horse myself; and *mine* he was, in fact, every hoof, vehicle and farming utensil on the Nest farm being as much my property, under the *old* laws, as the hat on my head" (236). The context for this remark is, of course, the antirent wars that threatened the holdings of landowners in New York State in the 1840s. But perhaps we should begin to inquire to what extent political arguments such as Cooper mounts in *The Redskins* are transmuted forms of a lifelong anxiety about possession.[3]

In Cooper's fiction, the "inside"—the protected space that lies at the center—is always subject to attack from the "outside." And it may be that all the threatened structures in his novels are ultimately symbolic of the threatened self, of the privileged but vulnerable interior space of the self. In many of the works in which such structures appear, Cooper carefully places them in settings whose isolation seems to make them secure. But an island environment of this kind—an "oasis amidst an ocean of wilderness" (164), as he calls the settlement in *The Wept of Wish-ton-Wish*—seldom remains safe for long.[4] In fact, the characteristic geological formation on which such structures rest—a "rise" or "knoll" within the center of a valley—is itself an expression of this paradox. On the one hand they are protected by their elevation, but on the other they are vulnerable because of their location in a valley. Regardless of how well

---

3. It is interesting to note that Cooper, like his father, did not support the rental system as such, preferring that small farmers be allowed to purchase their land. See David M. Ellis, "The Coopers and the New York State Land-holding Systems." His strong sympathy with the landowners in this dispute can be attributed, in part, to his sense of identification with their dispossession.

4. Cf. Frank M. Collins, "Cooper and the American Dream," p. 89.

these structures are fortified (many of them, even Tom Hutter's castle, are referred to as "fortresses"),[5] Cooper does not
allow us to think that the defenses will hold forever. For example, the "remote island" (119) of the Hutted Knoll in *Wyandotté*
(the "hut" is positioned on what was literally an island in the
center of a lake before the lake was drained) is heavily, even
elaborately, fortified, yet this does not prevent it from being
invaded and several of its inhabitants from being killed. In
novel after novel, Cooper's "islands" are subjected to attack
from the "outside." This pattern suggests that the writer felt a
compulsive need to continually reenact his deepest fears of
dispossession (in somewhat the same way in which Hemingway
felt the need to repeat the experience of the wound).

In *The Chainbearer,* the attack on valued structures is
mounted by Aaron Thousandacres, who declares his great joy
in " 'cuttin down trees . . . and cuttin', and slashin', and saw-
in' right and left, like all creation' " (285). The image is one of
wanton and uncontrollable destruction, destruction which will
leave behind a wasteland of stumps—a geography devoid of all
the natural demarcations that structure the space of the forest.
And this suggests the nature of Cooper's deepest fear. For
while the immediate threat is that forest or family estate will be
destroyed or stolen, the more frightening possibility is that the
very idea of boundary will be destroyed. Thousandacres is
not merely a destroyer of trees; he is an enemy of all forms of
human distinction. If he had his way, he would not only penetrate the boundary between "inside" and "outside" but elimi-
nate the very idea of boundary: " 'A Curse on all lines, in a free
country, say I' " (284). And for Cooper, a landscape without
demarcation (either natural or manmade) is a landscape of
chaos, even of nightmare. Andries Coejemans, the Chainbearer, is a valued member of Cooper's society precisely because he is the "man who measured land"; it is through his
agency as a boundary maker that Cooper's "holdings" are

5. Throughout his European travel journals and books, Cooper shows great
interest in fortified towns and structures.

protected. Coejemans is placed in direct contrast to Thousandacres, a figure "who took it [land] to himself without
measurement." Cooper tells us (as if the obviously symbolic
names did not) that the Chainbearer and Thousandacres represent "exactly antagonistic forces" (332).

As we have seen, the circle is the basic design in Cooper's
fictional world. The "beauty of curved lines" formalizes the
space of his parklike forests and represents the cyclical continuity of life in nature. But now we can also see how the circle
functions as a boundary. The clearing's edge that separates the
valley of the Wish-ton-Wish from the wilderness beyond is a
line of defense. More than that, it is a line which describes a
circle of possession; the narrator of *The Redskins*, Hugh Littlepage, owns all the land "for a circle of five miles around" (197).
But the circle—regardless of how it functions as an image in
Cooper's work—cannot withstand the attack from the "outside."

The axe in the hands of a figure like Thousandacres represents a serious threat to valued structures, but the greatest
destroyer in Cooper's fictional world is fire. His novels sometimes depict the warming, communal fire of the hearth or
Indian council, but the dominant form of fire in his work is
destructive, explosive, and volcanic. In Cooper's first American novel, *The Spy,* Harvey Birch's house is set aflame by the
rapacious Skinners, and later in the narrative the Wharton
home (the human structure that forms the center and organizes all of the novel's geography around it) is burned to the
ground. *The Spy* sets the pattern for the rest of Cooper's fiction.
In a large number of his thirty-two novels, some form of
human structure (house, hut, fort, blockhouse, settlement, or
ship) is destroyed or seriously threatened by fire, and often the
novel's climax is the moment of imminent conflagration. In
The Pioneers that moment occurs when one of the most valued
"structures" in Cooper's world, the forest, is set afire.

Fire is the most terrifying weapon at the command of those
who threaten from the "outside" because, of all the means of

attack they might employ, it is the only one which has the capacity to bring about total destruction; once ignited, it quickly becomes uncontrollable. The "smoldering ruin" of Fort William Henry in *The Last of the Mohicans* is an example of such destruction.

Mohicans is one of those works in which the incendiary force of the "outside" is represented by the Indian. (Also consider the Indian attempt to burn the blockhouse in *The Pathfinder* and the "torrent of fire" that threatens Natty and his companions in *The Prairie*.) But of the different groups which threaten from the "outside," the Indian was the most easily "contained" by the writer's imagination. Like Scott's Highlanders, Cooper's Indians figure in conflicts belonging to the past and can thus be treated in terms of romance. The struggle over the land that had taken place between the white settler and the Indian was essentially concluded in the East even by the time of Cooper's childhood. And we have seen how his Indians, both "good" and "bad," are given historical and cultural justification for their violent acts.

Furthermore, the destruction brought by the Indian, though apparently devastating, is never permanent. In *The Wept of Wish-ton-Wish,* Cooper describes the rebuilding of the settlement that had been burned to the ground by the Narragansetts. And the burning of Ben Boden's hut in *The Oak Openings* does not prevent Ben from returning to the same site later and developing a prosperous settlement. In *Satanstoe*, the first novel in the Littlepage trilogy, the defenders of Ravensnest are able to extinguish the fire set by the Indians and to drive the attackers away conclusively. But the two works that follow in the trilogy show that there were others whose incendiary actions would be far more difficult to contain. As the ironic title of *The Redskins* indicates, the worst threat that Cooper could imagine came from "Indians" with white skins. The white plunderers who first emerge in his fiction as the Skinners of *The Spy,* and who reappear throughout his work in different forms, are capable of utterly and permanently destroying an established structure.

Cooper imparts to these plunderers the "redskin" qualities of ferocity and destructiveness but gives them none of the real Indian's natural nobility. We can see him applying this distinction in a novel like *Wyandotté*, where the Hutted Knoll is threatened by marauders whose identity (white or red) is not clear for much of the narrative. In *The Redskins*, Cooper removes all doubt about the identity of the real destroyers and dramatizes the "redskin" (antirenter) attempt to burn down the long-established estate of Ravensnest. Hugh Littlepage, anticipating the attack of the "incendiaries" (398), expresses Cooper's deepest fear: " 'Fire is such a dreadful foe, and one is usually so helpless against its ravages in the country!' " (392).[6]

For Cooper, fire usually symbolizes passionate greed, the greed that makes society's "middle" an uncontrollable and dangerous force. In *Home as Found*, he suggests that the great New York City fire of 1835 can serve as an objectification (as well as a symbolic punishment) of the "temple of Mammon" that he felt New York had become. Just as "nothing [could] be done to arrest the flames" (127) of the New York fire, once it had been ignited, the destructive fires of Jacksonian America might be impossible to contain. Cooper gives these fires volcanic force in *The Redskins*; in that novel, he warns of the "volcano, which is raging and gathering strength beneath the whole community, menacing destruction to the nation itself" (407).

In his description of the New York fire in *Home as Found*, Cooper relates the hope of some that the great conflagration might result in "a better state of things," that "the community would, in a measure, be purified." He quickly adds, however, that "this expectation ended in disappointment, the infatuation being too widespread and corrupting to be stopped by

6. Part of the Three-Mile Point controversy involved the accidental burning by townspeople of a small house erected by William Cooper; see *L&J*, 4:270. Also see Susan Fenimore Cooper's account of her father's reaction to "the burning of the house at Fenimore" (*The Legends and Traditions of a Northern Country*, p. 214). In *Notions of the Americans*, Cooper describes the "dreary and savage" (1:255) appearance of land burned for logging.

even this check, and the rebuke was reserved for a form that seems to depend on a law of nature, that of causing a vice to bring with it its own infallible punishment" (128). But Cooper could not wait for nature to destroy the world he hated, and in *The Crater* he set out to do it himself.

The Crater recapitulates all the major issues of Cooper's fiction. The novel is his most literally conceived island setting, and the shores of Mark Woolston's paradise form an absolute boundary between the protected "inside" and the threatening "outside" to create an "Eden of modern times" (420). Shipwrecked on a mid-Pacific reef characterized by "dreariness" and "desolation" (67), Mark sets about the task of converting the island "from barrenness to fertility" (112). As his agricultural efforts on the floor of the crater prove successful, the reef gradually becomes "precious" (172) to him, just as Robinson Crusoe's island takes on value from work and accommodation to place. (*The Crater* shows the clear influence of Defoe's novel.) Ultimately, what had been to Mark a scene of desolation becomes a landscape of "the sweetest tranquillity and security" (139).

Then, as if in reward for his labors, a volcanic eruption brings a whole new and far more extensive world from the sea. Although Mark, like Robinson Crusoe, continues to cherish his original site more than the new territory, he is stunned by the beauty and plenitude of his acquisition. From a mountain peak on the northern end of the island (a peak that Cooper says strongly resembles the mysterious formation in Cole's *Course of Empire*), Mark surveys his island and takes almost palpable possession of it with the eye: "The whole plain of the island, with the exceptions of the covers made by intervening woods, lay spread before him like a map. All its beauties, its shades, its fruits, and its verdant glades, were placed beneath his eye, as if purposely to delight him with their glories" (199). As Mark explores "his new territories" (187)—the possessive pronoun is used consistently, and Cooper originally wanted to title the novel *Mark's Reef* (*L&J*, 5: 199, 215)—he begins the Adamic procedure of naming, giving value to geography by designating and demarcating its various elements: "Shell Bay" (188), "Cape North-East" (187), the "Prairie" (191). When Mark's fellow castaway, Bob Betts, returns from America with a few colonists, he brings Mark's young bride, Brigette, with him, and the edenic identification becomes explicit: "Then, he [Mark] had several times likened himself to Adam in the garden of Eden, before woman was given to him for a companion. Now, now he could feast his eyes on an Eve, who would have been highly attractive in any part of the world" (223).

In the early days of the little colony's growth, the characters inhabit an environment which has about it the aspect of permanence, of timelessness. Brigette roams "at pleasure over boundless fields, on which the grass was perennial . . . and among which numberless rills of the purest waters were sparkling like crystal" (226). Cooper describes the island setting as one of "eternal summer" (277) and depicts it in precisely those pastoral terms he typically applies to his most valued landscapes. Like the setting of *The Oak Openings*, the island's appearance suggests an "enchanting rural scene," and although it is virtually untouched by man, it possesses "the air of cultivation and art" (199–200).

Following the pattern established by Cooper's father in Cooperstown, Mark becomes the island's first political leader (its governor), a role he deserves because of his act of discovery and his initial labors. Under what amounts to his benevolent totalitarianism, the colony thrives, retaining in its newly civilized state its identification as a "garden of Eden" (255).

But in Cooper's work, Edens rarely remain islanded forever, and eventually the colonists must defend themselves from the forces of the "outside." First they are attacked by the hostile Waally savages (the Waallys correspond to Cooper's Mingoes, while friendly natives, the Ooroungs, remind us of the Delawares) and later by pirates. But these are the kinds of outside forces that Cooper's settlers usually manage, ultimately, to defeat. The greatest threat to the integrity of the island comes from those who have subtly crossed its boundary, those colonists who contain within them the "fires" of greed and passion. Despite Mark's attempts to limit his population and maintain stability—to hold his world in a state of permanence—order finally yields to chaos. The single religion Mark had insisted upon gives way to a situation in which "religion was running riot" (472). In politics too, factionalism develops and "revolution" (473) threatens. The emergence of the abhorred "majority principle" (473) means the displacement of Mark as governor, a development which confirms that the "little paradise" (200) is doomed.

The Crater is, of course, an allegory of the development of American society, and of the fate of the Cooper family within that society. And the volcanic destruction of Crater Island—it sinks beneath the sea—that concludes the novel is an act which punishes America for what it had done to the Cooper family. If Mark Woolston (read James Fenimore Cooper) cannot possess his world, then no one will. In Miles Wallingford, Cooper had written, "there must be a serious movement backward, or the nation is lost" (433). By the time he came to write The Crater, he seems to have recognized that such a movement was impossible.[7] The flames that (as Cooper suggests in Home as Found) once might have purified America now must destroy it. In The Crater, Cooper turns the volcanic flames of his enemies back upon themselves. The "internal fires" that had created the island now bring "a new convulsion, and the labors and hopes of years had vanished in a moment" (490–91). These are the fires of the final conflagration, of the apocalypse. We dream of them, Bachelard says, when we recognize that "we must disappear." Foreseeing our own destruction, we decide to "destroy the fire of our life by a superfire, by a super-human superfire without flame or ashes, which will bring extinction to the very heart of the being."[8]

---

7. Cf. Philbrick, "Introduction" to The Crater, p. xvii. For the darkest implications of Cooper's despair, see his late nautical tale, Jack Tier (1848), and social novel, The Ways of the Hour (1850).

8. The Psychoanalysis of Fire, p. 79. The volcano appears often as a metaphor

In one sense, the entire narrative that precedes the volcanic extinction of Crater Island is superfluous. Although there are indications that Cooper became absorbed in the act of depicting his island (*L&J*, 5: 215), we suspect as we read that he is creating a world for the singular purpose of destroying it. Parts of the novel—the sea voyage and the rendering of Mark's initial labors, in particular—are well executed, but the overall disjunctiveness, the pervasive didacticism, and a certain forced quality show how programmatic this effort was. What might have been one of Cooper's finest novels (the setting provides the materials with which he characteristically did his best work) becomes a mere vehicle for ideas.

Cooper uses *The Crater* to attack every contemporary abuse he can think of—the irresponsibility of newspapers, political and religious factionalism, mob rule, and social and educational experimentation. Because the novelist's anger is so close to the surface, and because the urge to rebuke is so strong, Cooper's island experience is irreparably damaged. The writer, failing to respect the world he has made, becomes the most intrusive and destructive "outsider" in the novel. Far more than any of his fictional plunderers, Cooper himself robs this paradise of its integrity.

The Crater has the appearance of a world forced into being (and then forced into oblivion) to prove a point. Unlike Cooper's most compelling island settings, this one has the quality of a world "made" rather than of a world "found." When, at the beginning of *The Deerslayer*, Leatherstocking and the reader see the Glimmerglass for the first time, we experience a moment of genuine discovery, a moment which fully conveys the joy of the first impression. *The Deerslayer* is not a world "found" in the sense of the word as it is used in the title of *Home as Found* (another novel, like *The Crater*, which uses both

in Cooper's writings. For example, describing the unstable political climate in France, he says, "France is a Volcano" (*L&J*, 2:240); and in *The Pioneers*, Oliver Effingham's anger toward Judge Temple is rendered in this way: "the volcano burst its boundaries" (380).

setting and character for didactic purposes),[9] where it means re-found in a sullied state. Rather, *The Deerslayer* is a world just-found, a world found-just-now. And as we have seen, Cooper discovered the setting of this novel in the region of his own childhood memories and not, as was the case with *The Crater*, in reading the Pacific travel literature of his time.

Perhaps *The Crater* does not succeed, either as a social experiment or as a work of art, because its boundaries are not secure enough. Although it is certainly one of the most isolated of Cooper's island settings, it is bounded only by space. And space alone is never sufficient to prevent the attack from the "outside." Although Mark Woolston makes every effort to hold his world in a state that is timeless and permanent, its temporal location in the early nineteenth century makes it vulnerable to the onslaught of the modern, the onslaught of history itself.

Cooper's most compelling "islands" are those protected not only by spatial barriers but also by the barrier of time. The world of *The Deerslayer* is sealed off by a "belt of forest which inclosed it, as it might be hermetically" (83). The mountains that surround it act as "barriers to exclude the outer world" (440). But what most renders it "a world by itself" (157) is its location at the very beginning of American history. Perhaps it is even more temporally remote than that, for it suggests a time *before* history. (*The Deerslayer* communicates a quality of timelessness distinguishing it from Cooper's more "historical" works, even though some of these, such as *The Wept of Wish-ton-Wish*, are set in earlier periods.) This is the significance of the fact that the concluding passage describes a world totally unchanged fifteen years after the events enacted in the novel. *The Deerslayer* renders an authentic sense of what Bachelard calls the "permanence of childhood," the permanence of "an immobile time."[10] It is a self-contained world of the imagina-

9. For Cooper's purposes in writing *Homeward Bound* and *Home as Found*, see *L&J*, 4:274.

10. *The Poetics of Reverie*, pp. 133, 192.

tion, a "cosmos," produced by reverie. As D. H. Lawrence said of the novel, "From the first words we pass straight into the world of sheer creation, with so perfect a transit that we are unconscious of our translation."[11]

This is not to say that the novel is devoid of references to the threat of history. Certainly, in the figure of Thomas Hutter, Cooper characterizes one of the archetypal despoilers of his imagination. But *The Deerslayer* differs from a work like *The Crater* in that the full force of history is never allowed to break in. Despite Hutter's destructive impulses, characterized by his and Harry March's unsuccessful expedition to scalp Hurons for bounty, there is nothing he can do to violate the pastoral. He is utterly contained by the setting and in his death is absorbed by it. Remotely but importantly, Hutter is related to Judge Marmaduke Temple as a father/maker of civilizations. But unlike Temple, whose uncontested power in *The Pioneers* makes that a novel *about* the father, Hutter is a figure without power or moral authority. As we saw earlier, *The Deerslayer* is a world in which the "child" dominates, and a childhood imagination controls the narrative. Cooper effectively nullifies the power of the father (the adult, or the reality principle) by rendering him hopelessly corrupt.

In *The Deerslayer*, Leatherstocking's only competition for the beautiful Judith Hutter is Harry March, a moral copy of Hutter, so that the human setting, like the physical one, radiates pure wish fulfillment. Deerslayer, of course, cannot marry, but the fact that he could have Judith if he wanted is perfectly in keeping with the fantasy. This is the novel, as Cooper wrote in a letter, in which Leatherstocking *"is beloved"* (*L&J*, 4: 112). In the deep logic of the narrative, Judith's love of Deerslayer is made possible by her total rejection of her (foster) father. And only in a novel of this kind could the fantasy of childhood be allowed to come so close to the surface. Only with Hutter so thoroughly corrupted (hence displaced) could Judith be allowed to exclaim, " 'I sometimes wish I had no father!' "

11. *The Symbolic Meaning*, p. 106.

(288)—a statement which does more than signal the disclosure that Hutter is but a stepfather.

But Judith too, in a different way, is also a despoiler. Unlike her childlike sister Hetty, she possesses an adult sexuality disapproved of by (and perhaps frightening to) both Deerslayer and Cooper.[12] Because sexuality is one of those forces of the "outside" that exist beyond the boundaries of childhood, the writer must remove Judith just as he removes Thomas Hutter, and he does so in a similar way. Hutter is undercut as a father-figure because he is corrupt; Judith is rendered not only fully sexual but also morally tainted, and Cooper leaves no doubt that it is this moral taint which forces her to leave the Glimmerglass for a form of exile in Europe. Finally, the Glimmerglass is saved, preserved, from all forms of adult intrusion.

The Deerslayer, like *The Pioneers*, is a symbolic journey to Cooper's childhood home. But *The Deerslayer* is a return to a better home than that depicted in *The Pioneers*. Although Lawrence's formulation does not apply as well as he thought to all five of the Leatherstocking tales, it certainly applies to the movement from *The Pioneers* to *The Deerslayer*: "a *decrescendo* of reality, and a crescendo of beauty."[13] It is a movement from reality to dream, from "difficulty" to simplicity, from a world dominated by the father (the "Judge") to a world dominated by the child. *The Deerslayer* is a book touched by reverie and aestheticized by the imagination.

After seven years in Europe, Cooper made a "pilgrimage to the scene[s?] of my youth and childhood" (*L&J*, 3: 12) and sent his first impressions to his wife: "The lake looks larger, the mountains lower than I had expected" (*L&J*, 3: 43). The reaction is disappointment, explainable in part by the fact that Cooper had recently returned from a Europe of small mountain lakes and the magnificent Alps and may have made an

12. Perhaps this is why, although many readers of Cooper's time preferred Judith to Hetty, Cooper himself confessed, "Hetty is my own favorite" (*L&J*, 4:308). As he makes explicit in the novel, Hetty is childlike in the same way as Deerslayer.

13. *Studies in Classic American Literature*, p. 50.

unconscious comparison. But perhaps there is a better explanation. Isn't it possible that in Cooper's childhood memories,
those most deeply engraved of our memories, Otsego was a
concentrated jewel of precious fluid, smaller, more condensed
than the real lake? And the mountains may have been "lower"
for him because in childhood memory, as Bachelard says, "the
hill gets bigger. . . . The little becomes big. The world of
childhood reverie is as big, bigger than the world offered to
today's reverie. From poetic reverie, inspired by some great
spectacle of the world to childhood reverie, there is a com-
merce of grandeur." "And that is why," Bachelard explains,
"childhood is at the origin of the greatest landscapes." [14] And
that is also why the majestic mountains rising above the Glimmerglass in *The Deerslayer* are "bigger" than the real mountains
surrounding Lake Otsego.

14. *The Poetics of Reverie,* p. 102.

10

Satanstoe: The Case for Permanence

> [We] recognize within the human soul the permanence of
> a nucleus of childhood, an immobile but ever living child-
> hood, outside history, hidden from the others, disguised
> in history when it is recounted, but which has real being
> only in its instants of illumination which is the same as
> saying in the moment of its poetic existence.
>
> Gaston Bachelard, *The Poetics of Reverie*

The Deerslayer and *The Crater* have the same spatial design (both
depict "islands" surrounded by a vast wilderness), yet one
novel describes a world poised in an idyllic moment while the
other communicates a too urgent sense of danger. As a result, the "boundedness" of *The Deerslayer* becomes the
"boundary"—fiercely defended—of *The Crater*. As we have
seen, the world of *The Deerslayer* is protected not only by a
spatial barrier but also by time; it is isolated in a moment of the
nation's prehistory, a time before American history is set in
motion. *The Crater*, on the other hand, is Cooper's ambitious
and dogmatic attempt to allegorize the entire drama of America's course of empire—its past, present, and future. The writer
allows time to flow into his paradise and to destroy it as a way of
exposing his enemies to attack.

Cooper's dominant tendency was to confront these enemies
directly, and much of his fiction has a strongly argumentative
quality. But there are among his works several novels which
demonstrate the capacity to stand back from the battle. For
example, the three romances written at the beginning of the
1840s (*The Pathfinder, The Deerslayer,* and the sea novel, *Wing-
and-Wing*) all reveal the wish, as Thomas Philbrick has said, to

"retreat from the oppressive reality of here and now."[1] Books
like these suggest a temporary withdrawal from direct confrontation with the political and social issues that Cooper
treated vigorously in the fiction of the 1830s and, with different emphasis, in the novels of the later 1840s. They appear
to have been written in the interstices of his struggles, in
periods when the polemicist in him was at rest.

To see Cooper's pastoral novels in this light is to regard them
as almost fortuitous, happy accidents that resulted from the
need to find respite in the world of the romance. The
emergence of a book like *The Deerslayer* would seem to depend
upon such an accident, one produced by the coincidence of two
closely related conditions: a diminishing of the writer's desire
to instruct his countrymen, and his choice of a time setting that
prevents the intrusion of history. Yet Cooper wrote one remarkable book which forces us to extend the dimensions and
define more fully the dynamics of his pastoralism. For *Satanstoe*
is a most compelling pastoral novel that was written with
polemical intent and whose moment is set in history.

Social and intellectual historians have been attracted to the
Littlepage novels as a group because of the ideas they
dramatize. But *Satanstoe* deserves to be treated on its own terms
for, aesthetically, it stands apart from the didactic works that
fill out the trilogy. Unlike *The Deerslayer*, it stands at the beginning of its series not only in respect to time setting but also in
the order of composition. When Cooper published the first of
the Leatherstocking tales (*The Pioneers*) in 1823, he was not
planning a five-part series. And when he concluded *The Prairie*
(1827) with Natty Bumppo's death, he felt he had put his
character to rest for good. The resumption of the tales in the
1840s with *The Pathfinder* and *The Deerslayer* reveals several
obvious discontinuities. In contrast, the Littlepage trilogy was

---

1. *James Fenimore Cooper and the Development of American Sea Fiction*, p. 127.
Another sea novel from an earlier period which communicates a sense of pure
romance is *The Water Witch* (1830). Written in Italy, a country which seems to
have relaxed Cooper's rigid sensibilities, it obeys all the principles of the
author's pastoralism. See my essay, "A Repossession of America."

designed as a composite statement about American society, and the three novels that comprise the series were written together, out of a preconceived narrative plan.

Cooper described this plan in a letter to his publisher. "The Family of Littlepage," he said, would "form three complete Tales, each perfectly distinct from the other as regards leading characters, love story &c," but connected by the fact that he would carry "the same family, the same localities, and same *things* generally through the three different books, but exhibiting the changes produced by time." As we saw earlier, Cooper regarded the Revolution as the event that had exposed (white) America to the full force of history. In this letter, he refers to the first book in the series as "Colony" and to the second as "Revolution," suggesting that *The Chainbearer* would describe the changes produced by time in the immediate postrevolutionary era. This second novel, Cooper went on, would depict a setting "in some respects resembling the Pioneers," a setting, in other words, characterized by the destructive forces of the settlement stage. The third novel, "Republic" (*The Redskins*), would treat "the present aspect of things, with an exhibition of the Anti-Rent commotion that now exists among us, and which certainly threatens the destruction of our system" (*L&J*, 5: 7).

Cooper intended, then, that *Satanstoe* would depict the nation's colonial youth, a time before the rapacious forces of the "outside" had gained strength. In *The Chainbearer* and *The Redskins*, he would show the damage being inflicted upon the world founded (and "found") in the first novel. Here we have a rare case in which the deliberateness of the writer's plan worked to aesthetic advantage, for in *Satanstoe* Cooper set out to create a pastoral, the ease and beauty of which would shame the turbulence and ugliness of later periods. Remarkably, he succeeded. In this novel, we do not hear the strident and intrusive voice of the social novels, in part because the writer knew he had reserved the opportunity to argue openly in the two later works. That is, by dramatizing the rise and fall of the landed gentry (on whose welfare Cooper believed America's destiny depended) in three separate novels, he avoided the necessity of forcing an entire historical development into one epic narrative, as he had done in *The Crater*. And perhaps it is also true that the first-person narration allowed him to inhabit the spirit of the ingenuous Corny Littlepage and to relax into the world of the romance.

Satanstoe, then, describes a simpler and more beautiful past, and the effect is similar to that of *The Deerslayer*. Yet different means are used to gain this effect, and the moments these two novels depict are not the same. While *The Deerslayer* focuses upon the adventures of a simple woodsman in a setting so isolated that it seems to exist "before" history, *Satanstoe* records the entry of America's gentry class into the affairs of national life. In the words of the young narrator-hero, the novel describes that moment when, "for the first time in the history of the colonies, the Littlepages had become the owners of what might be termed an estate" (157).

Although the old family home of Satanstoe (near colonial New York City) is cherished by the Littlepage family, the unclaimed Mooseridge estate in the wilderness represents the *new* country Americans would possess for themselves after the Revolution. Therefore, Corny Littlepage's journey "in quest of the patent" (156), and Herman Mordaunt's parallel venture from his Hudson River home (Lilacsbush) to the wilderness settlement of Ravensnest, dramatize the initial stage of America's journey into the future.

That *Satanstoe* is organized by a symbolic journey suggests its relationship to *The Last of the Mohicans*. Both these novels describe a movement from a known world to the unknown northern wilderness, and, as Cooper notes in the letter cited above, they are set in the same period (the late 1750s) and region (the characters in *Satanstoe* pass by the ruin of Fort William Henry). But as we shall see, the similarity of structure and the intersection of time and place do not amount to a true correspondence. While the basic issue of both works—and of all of Cooper's fiction—is possession, *Satanstoe* is as different from *The Last of the Mohicans* as *The Deerslayer* is from *The Crater*. Just as Cooper could create an "island" that remained pro-

tected from the forces of destruction, he could also narrate a
journey that was not characterized by "difficulty."

In every way, *Satanstoe* renders the sense of a beginning. The
"journey to the north" (144) commences on March first, with
spring about to break. Corny informs his readers that "winter
was soon drawing to a close, and my twenty-first birthday was
past" (156). This coincidence of the journey's beginning and
Corny's coming of age signifies a parallel between the young
hero's and the nation's development, a parallel of rich association which we shall examine shortly. Before the expedition can
begin, however, Cooper must first describe the family home of
Satanstoe, for it is from this original site and its surrounding
landscape that the journey draws its momentum. The first ten
chapters of the novel treat in great detail and with "a loving
sense of fact" [2] the charming ways and quaint manners of the
prerevolutionary New York City region. But the most important background these early chapters provide is their rendering of Corny Littlepage's idyllic development through childhood to the moment of departure.

The circumstances of this fictional childhood suggest that,
through Corny, the writer is offering an idealized version of
his own growth, and it may be that this is the youth Cooper
would have lived. There is much in the novel to indicate the
author's origins, and many of the details, such as Corny's
tutorship under an "English divine" (26),[3] are strictly autobiographical. It is true that the setting is removed from the
Cooperstown region, yet this may be merely a displacement
allowing a highly self-conscious writer to particularize the rest
of the setting as his own.

In a voice which is self-promoting even as it pretends self-
effacement, the narrator describes the highly favorable cir-

    2. Richard Chase, *The American Novel and Its Tradition, Vision*, p. 51. Cf. A. N.
Kaul, *The American Vision*, p. 90.
    3. In the fall of his eleventh year, Cooper was sent from Cooperstown to
Albany to study with a clergyman whose allegiance to his native England was
strong.

cumstances of his growing up. Born into prominence and wealth, properly educated (unlike Cooper, he graduates from college), the pride of his extended family, Corny represents himself as "special." As if to confirm this status, Cooper (the twelfth of thirteen children born into his family) makes his character a beloved only child. Although there "was a son who preceded me, and two daughters succeeded," Corny explains, "they all died in infancy, leaving me in effect the only offspring for my parents to cherish and educate" (15). Corny's "tender-hearted" mother is "full of anxiety in behalf of an only child" (58), and almost everyone in the novel, including the great Lord Howe (370), takes note of this fact about him—thus suggesting his crucial importance to his family's destiny.

We have seen how in *The Deerslayer* the father figure is rendered powerless by making him corrupt. In *Satanstoe*, there is only a hint of this—Corny's father "had the reputation of a gadabout" (57)—but the displacement is just as effective. It is hard to imagine a novel concerning the destiny of a family in which the father is more invisible. Much attention is given to Corny's loving relationship with his mother—as in *The Deerslayer*, a maternal presence pervades the world of the book—but the father is barely acknowledged. As we shall see, certain "pioneering" aspects of the paternal role are transferred to the heroine's father, Herman Mordaunt. But at another level, Corny himself takes this role. That is, he "fathers" the Littlepage destiny by exploring and helping to secure the Mooseridge and Ravensnest estates. It is to him as the founder that all subsequent generations will look back with reverence. Cooper himself was acutely aware that, though he had "embellished [Otsego Hall] a little," it was his father, William Cooper, who had "founded the place, and it is the first man who becomes identified with any thing of this sort" (*L&J*, 5: 369). Perhaps, through Corny Littlepage, Cooper imaginatively becomes "the first man" and gathers to himself the full identification he may have (unconsciously) desired. This interpretation, however, is less important to our analysis than the narrative implications of Corny's role as founder, a role which places him at the absolute center of the novel's stage.

Despite his heavy responsibility as the carrier of his family's destiny, Corny's is a life remarkably free of disruption and protected from the tragedy that Cooper himself knew in childhood.[4] In *Satanstoe*, the writer appears to have taken the basic facts of his youth and imposed upon them an order and felicity which his own life (or any real life) could not sustain. Cooper seems to invest Corny's development with all of those things that, as an aging author, he had come to value. For example, he makes his character an Episcopalian from birth, thereby giving him the religion to which he himself became committed only much later.[5] Similarly, Corny's wooing of Anneke Mordaunt—recognizable as an analogue of Cooper's own romance with Susan DeLancey[6]—is a case of giving to the entire span of the character's life those "treasures" that came to the writer only in increments. Cooper extends this romance all the way back into Corny's childhood and allows his child-hero to save Anneke from both a bully and a circus lion. Such episodes suggest wish fulfillment, and they demonstrate the way in which Cooper idealizes his character's development and spares him from "difficulty."

The ten chapters, then, that precede the "journey to the north" are more than preliminary. They describe both Corny's and his region's idyllic past and communicate the love the hero feels for his childhood home of Satanstoe. When the journey begins, we experience no sudden departure from that valued past; rather, the quality of amenity established in the first section of the novel is carried forward and informs all of the events the narrative will bring. Thus, while one of the purposes of the journey is to test Corny's emerging manhood, it is a test so lovingly and carefully managed by the author that its out-

4. Cooper's beloved sister Hannah died tragically when he was ten years old. Her death was a loss from which he never fully recovered. See *L&J*, 6:99.

5. Cooper, whose father was of Quaker background, became active in Episcopal diocesan affairs in his later life and was confirmed by the church shortly before his death.

6. Cooper met and fell in love with Susan DeLancey after returning from naval service. In *Satanstoe*, he seems to invest Anneke Mordaunt's home, Lilacsbush, with his affection for the DeLancey mansion at Mamaroneck, N.Y.

come is never in doubt. Although this novel ostensibly treats a
character's growth, there is no development in the modern
sense. Corny simply becomes what he was destined to become,
and while he travels into regions unknown to him, he never
really leaves the landscape of home.

It is entirely in keeping with the spirit of *Satanstoe* that the
journey into the wilderness is delayed by a sustained and beautiful interlude in colonial Albany. Dutch geniality pervades this
scene of feasting, young love, and adventure.[7] Most importantly, Albany provides the setting for the development of the
romance between Corny and Anneke. The young suitor must
prove himself a man, and, as we saw in *The Pathfinder*, women
are always the final arbiters of adulthood in Cooper's fiction.
When Anneke discovers Corny and his friend Guert Ten Eyck
sledding playfully, her sarcastic refusal to join them makes her
role clear: " 'when Miss Wallace or I wish to ride down hill, and
become little girls again, we will trust ourselves with boys,
whose constant practice will be likely to render them more
expert than men can be, who have had time to forget the habits
of their childhood' " (193). The issue, then, is Corny's growth
from childhood to maturity, and this growth will be measured
by events. Corny, of course, does prove his manhood—most
conclusively by saving Anneke from a terrifying upheaval of
ice on the Hudson, an event which in several ways is the
climactic, and most skillfully rendered, scene of the novel. Yet
this heroic act is not qualitatively different from those rescues
Corny performed earlier in childhood. Together, they form a
continuum, and it is hard to locate a moment of genuine
initiation (later scenes in which Corny fights bravely against
French troops and a party of hostile Indians have a largely
perfunctory quality). But Cooper clearly intends that we regard the ice scene as a major turning point in the hero's
development (and in his relationship to Anneke), and as readers we accept this even as we realize how carefully this de-

7. The Dutch give this same quality of geniality to *The Water Witch*. Cf.
Washington Irving's and James K. Paulding's treatment of the Dutch.

velopment has been controlled. As if to affirm the continuity of
his character's growth, Cooper has Anneke tell Corny at the
novel's conclusion that she has never loved anyone but him,
even from childhood. His success was never in doubt, and all
that was required of him was to carry through his preordained
destiny. Corny remains as earnest and naive at the novel's
conclusion as he was at the beginning. His maturation has been
formal rather than developmental; it exhibits none of the
turbulence and pain of adolescence, only the tranquillity of an
"immobile" childhood.

On one level, Anneke's rejection of the suave and aggressive
Major Bulstrode symbolizes Cooper's rejection of English
influence in American life. But on another, Bull-strode's name
as well as his behavior indicate that he represents an adult
sexuality which the writer excludes from this world of romance. Just as much as *The Deerslayer*, *Satanstoe* is a novel
dominated by the spirit of childhood. Although Corny differs
in many significant ways from Natty Bumppo, his character is
as essentially fixed. Like Leatherstocking, he remains childlike
after his (formal) initiation. The effect of immutability is
heightened by the first-person narration, for Corny's voice,
even in the retrospective, adult position from which he tells his
story, remains that of the innocent—a voice Cooper more than
once treats with affectionate and humorous irony.

From every point of view, this is Corny's story. He narrates it
himself, and in the fullest sense he is the "only child" of
Satanstoe—the true center of the narrative.[8] The great public
events of the novel take on importance primarily as they figure
in his personal destiny. In *The Last of the Mohicans*, we saw how
personal destinies were overwhelmed by massive historical
forces, but in *Satanstoe* such forces are contained, even or-

8. Cooper had various thematic purposes in mind in killing off the attractive
and amiable Guert Ten Eyck, but certainly one of them was to allow Corny to
dominate the novel's conclusion totally. There is a hint of guilt in Corny's
remark, "I could have called out to warn them [Guert and his companions] of
the danger they ran; but it would have done no good, nor was there time for
remonstrances" (464).

ganized to accommodate the hero's development. This contrast is most obvious in Cooper's use and treatment of the
"great historical event" in these two novels. The massacre of
Fort William Henry in *The Last of the Mohicans* is so violent that
it breaks the narrative in half and turns its journey in an
entirely new direction. Yet the comparable event in *Satanstoe*,
the French defeat of the English at Fort Ticonderoga, has a
very different function. Although Cooper vividly depicts its
violence and suffering, the great battle is not a climactic turning point. Rather, the scene of war is just that, a "scene," one
which diverts our attention only briefly from the major movement of the novel. Corny's and Guert's expedition to join the
British forces, after they have located the Mooseridge estate,
has the quality of an excursion. The military action serves
primarily as a demonstration of these characters' valor; their
personal victory in a skirmish with the enemy is given far more
attention than the historically significant event of the British
defeat.[9] In fact, the routing of the English troops prompts the
impulsive Guert to disassociate himself (and Corny) from the
whole effort, which he now sees as discredited: " 'My advice is,
t'at we get out of this army as we got into it—t'at is, py a
one-sided movement' " (380). It is by just such a one-sided, or
lateral, movement that the characters exit from the scene of the
great historical event and return to their central pursuit, the
securing of the Mooseridge and Ravensnest estates. After this
exit, we hear no more about the French and Indian Wars; the
battle becomes an experience which Corny may someday relate
to nis grandchildren.

Yet this is not to say that *Satanstoe* lacks historical meaning.
Although Corny's personal destiny dominates our vision, this
destiny intersects and symbolizes the nation's. The "journey to
the north" is America's journey too, and the writer controls its
progress just as carefully as he controls the hero's development.

9. Cf. Harry B. Henderson, 3rd, *Versions of the Past*, p. 81.

The Littlepage and Mordaunt families represent the class of Americans upon whom Cooper centered his greatest hopes for social stability. Therefore, these families' acquisition of property in the unknown northern wilderness signifies a claim upon the future and the establishment of a substantial base for America's growth. But it is important to add that the wilderness explored by the *Satanstoe* characters is unknown in only a limited sense. This is not the geography of the second journey of *The Last of the Mohicans*, a mythic region beyond the demarcations of civilization. Corny Littlepage and Herman Mordaunt do not probe the unknown; rather, they "discover" what they already (legally) possess, in the same way that Corny "becomes" what he already is. The boundary lines of their estates had been drawn long before the time period of the novel; the purpose of the journey is to locate these lines, to lay claim to what has already been recorded on the patent. Although it requires the intuition of an Indian guide to find the Mooseridge estate, Cooper's clear intention is to show that even here, in this apparently wild setting, boundaries exist. Wherever prior claims have been made, possession is inviolate—except, of course, in the case of the Indian, whose dispossession Cooper regarded as tragic but necessary (in this novel, the bitter voice of Susquesus reminds us of that dispossession).

As the identifying landmark of the Mooseridge estate is first seen, we experience the characteristic moment of appropriation in Cooper's fiction, the moment when the eye gathers its possessions. We suddenly know we have come to "the end of our journey" (343), and the act of appropriation is confirmed by "the erection of a log-house" (344). The site for this "hut" (347) is chosen because "water was abundant and good, and because a small knoll was near the spring" (345). These formations identify this place immediately as the center of Cooper's imaginative geography, the generative site from which a civilization can grow. Like Ben Boden's shanty in *The Oak Openings*, or Captain Willoughby's first primitive dwelling in *Wyandotté*, the Mooseridge hut will serve as a "citadel to retreat to" (346), until more substantial structures can be raised.

While Mooseridge is being marked off as a site for future development (and, ultimately, sale), Herman Mordaunt vigorously and quickly establishes a full-scale settlement at nearby Ravensnest. As I suggested earlier, Mordaunt is the prototypal maker of civilizations in Cooper's fiction—strong, decisive, enterprising. Yet in *Satanstoe* the writer shows toward this figure none of the ambivalence revealed in *The Pioneers*. Mordaunt is the paternal landholder whose protective attitude toward his settlers is convincingly demonstrated during the Indian attack on Ravensnest.

The siege of Ravensnest reminds us of scenes in several of Cooper's other novels. As in *The Wept of Wish-ton-Wish*, the Indians' most dangerous weapon is fire, but whereas fire totally destroys the settlement in the earlier work, here it is extinguished before it can do harm. In fact, the defenders of Ravensnest control the flames from the beginning. They watch an Indian warrior set the fire, allow it to burn at the base of the fortress for a time because its light exposes the enemy to rifle fire, and then easily extinguish it with water. When we compare this image of easily contained fire with Cooper's characteristic depiction of a rapidly and totally consuming fire, we suspect that in *Satanstoe* the writer is "playing" with the element he feared most—further evidence of the book's pervasive authorial control. But the containment of fire also symbolizes the fact that the Indian is already an anachronistic force in the time and place of this setting (unlike the setting of *The Wept of Wish-ton-Wish*, in which he is an everpresent danger). Although Corny fears, in the confusion of night, that "we must be surrounded by hundreds of these ruthless foes" (456), the daylight reveals that this is but an isolated band which, once driven away, will never return. The victory of Corny and his friends is conclusive, and the narrator leaves no doubt that now the process of settlement will go on uninterrupted by Indian attack.

Later in history, Ravensnest will be "interrupted" again by

far more dangerous "redskins." In *Satanstoe*, Cooper warns of
this future danger, but as in *The Deerslayer*, he introduces the
rapacious forces of the "outside" only in order to contain them.
"Outside," in this case, is New England; the boundary between
"the colony of New York and those that lie east of the Byram
River" is characterized as "a broad moral line" (17). Cooper
believed that Calvinism in New England had bred acquisitiveness, and many of the destructive figures in his fiction are of
New England origin.[10] In *Satanstoe*, the invader from Connecticut is Jason Newcome, whose manners reveal how little he
understands of "the fitness of things." Jason ignores, or tries to
ignore, all distinctions between "rank, education, birth and
experience" (326). His name identifies him as a trespasser
(Newcome) and also as a thief (Jason) who would steal the
Littlepage and Mordaunt "treasure"; he openly reveals his
designs on Herman Mordaunt's property. But at this moment
in history he is unable to enact his desire, for in *Satanstoe* the
power is gathered on the side of the gentry. Later, in an
America which Cooper saw endangered by the common man,
legal distinctions would break down and boundaries would be
crossed with impunity. Jason's presence in this novel represents the first intrusion of the "outside," and his own as well as
his descendants' influence will grow to dangerous proportions
in later periods represented in *The Chainbearer* and *The Redskins*
(in the latter novel, Jason's grandson attempts to burn the
Ravensnest estate). But in *Satanstoe*, Cooper contains these
forces just as he contains the Indians' fire; Jason is rendered
ineffectual, even laughable. Like Thomas Hutter in *The
Deerslayer*, he represents the potential, rather than the reality,
of spoliation and does not immediately threaten Cooper's
"island."

It is true that at points throughout the novel, and again on
the final pages, the "difficulties" of the future are predicted.
But as in *The Deerslayer*, the integrity of the island experience is
never violated, either by fictional marauders or by Cooper

10. See McAleer, "Biblical Analogy in the Leatherstocking Tales," passim.
Also see Cooper's severe attack on Puritanism in *The Wept of Wish-ton-Wish*.

himself. Instead, the distant threat to the island adds a precariousness to the moment of the novel without disturbing its
idyllic quality. We know that the world depicted in *Satanstoe* will
not remain intact forever, yet Cooper allows the narrative to
close without introducing the destruction brought by history.
The Revolution and its accompanying turbulence and disloca-
tion are still almost two decades away. The novel concludes not
on a note of "difficulty" but with a sense of secure possession.
By marrying Anneke (who is, like Corny, an only child and
therefore the sole inheritor of her family's wealth), the young
hero takes possession of her estate as well as his own. Thus the
Littlepages and Mordaunts become "one family" (501), their
holdings consolidated.

Yet there is another consolidation at least as important as
this. For the journey into the wilderness has also joined
Satanstoe to Mooseridge and Lilacsbush to Ravensnest, which
is to say that the past has been linked to the future. Cooper
believed that every historical advance must be related significantly to preexisting patterns and values. The joining of the
old estates to the new, with an established American family in
control of the transition, symbolizes the ideal of cultural continuity. Cooper's futuring, or westering, is not that of the
pioneer, but that of the settler, in the fullest sense of the term.[11]
It is entirely fitting, therefore, that the novel concludes with a
return to the world of Satanstoe and Lilacsbush; this is the
significance of the title, which at first may appear inappropriate. For *Satanstoe* is a book about the value of "the old place"
(494), and the "return to Satanstoe" (493) is, from this point of
view, the most important journey of the novel. It enacts the
rhythm of continuity, the full circle of return to the center and,
significantly, to the mother: "My dear mother," Corny relates,
"hugged me to her heart again and again, and seemed never to
be satisfied with feasting her eyes on me" (491). Unlike *The Last
of the Mohicans*, *Satanstoe* does not conclude with the characters
stranded in a ruptured moment of history in the deepest of

---

11. See Sidney Mead's distinction between pioneers and settlers in "The
American People: Their Space, Time, and Religion," *The Lively Experiment*.

America's wilderness. Rather, Cooper dramatizes in this novel the full return that was aborted in the earlier work.

Furthermore, the "distance" between the world explored and the world returned to is not great. While *The Last of the Mohicans* describes an irreconcilable difference between its polar geographies, the imagery of *Satanstoe* suggests union rather than division. Like *The Oak Openings*, this novel works toward a complementary rather than an oppositional relationship between civilization and nature. Corny sees Anneke's Hudson River home as "a wilderness of shrubbery" (490). Correspondingly, the "canopied space" (408) of the real wilderness contains all those valued shapes and structures that make Cooper's forest a home. And, as we have seen, the wilderness of *Satanstoe* is not the undiscovered country of *The Last of the Mohicans* but is instead a region already plotted and appropriated by the human imagination.

The return to Satanstoe, "with all its endearing ties" (490), and to "the peace and security of Lilacsbush" (443), closes the circle of the novel's action and dramatizes the centripetal force of the writer's pastoralism. Cooper always gravitates imaginatively toward an island of space which contains his most valued possessions. Such an island of "eulogized space" is defined by what Bachelard calls "its protective value." It is the kind of space "that may be grasped, that may be defended against adverse forces, the space we love." [12] In *Satanstoe*, Cooper holds and protects this island by identifying it with his own and the nation's childhood. Cooper and the reader are returned to the landscape of home, even as the novel points toward the promise (and danger) of the future. The journey draws a circle around the fictional experience of the book and serves the same function as the perimeter of the lake in *The Deerslayer*. This is a different kind of spatial boundary from that provided by the Glimmerglass, but it just as effectively excludes "the outer world."

The structure of *Satanstoe* also creates a temporal boundary. Begun in late winter and completed in midsummer, the novel's

12. *The Poetics of Space*, p. xxxi.

journey depicts the nation's springtime, a time when "the buds [were] just breaking into the first green of foliage" (332). Cooper's achievement is to make this springtime a permanent fact of the imagination by framing it in a timeless moment. Although *Satanstoe* dramatizes the first stage of America's journey into the future, its temporal quality is essentially ahistorical. Just as Corny does not develop as a character, the novel's circular motion encloses its action in a narrative framework that protects it from time. The form of the trilogy provides further protection, for the back cover of the book separates its fictional space from that of *The Chainbearer* and *The Redskins*. The world of *Satanstoe* is forfeited in the two later works, but it preserves itself in our imaginations through a convincing rendering of a state of permanence.

On the final pages, Corny defends "permanent principles" and attacks the New England "craving for change" (495). He is troubled, he says, by a tendency among figures like Jason Newcome to alter place names: "I love old names, such as my father knew the same places by. . . . So it is with Satanstoe; the name is homely . . . but it is strong and conveys an idea. It relates also to the usages and notions of the country; and names ought always to be preserved" (494).[13] The real issue here is theft, for if Satanstoe's name were to be "frittered away" (495) by the likes of Jason Newcome, its essential identity would also be lost. The loss of the name is the first step in the loss of the thing itself, and Cooper's great fear was that social instability, brought about by "outsiders" such as Jason, would rob him of all the things he valued. This is why he felt compelled to conclude *Satanstoe* with a soliloquy by Corny on the importance of "permanent principles." Yet the speech is hardly necessary, for the novel itself has presented a far more convincing case for permanence. It describes a world of abundance, grace, and charm made secure by its location in the valued past.

13. Cooper often complained of changes in place names. For example, see *The Sea Lions,* pp. 488–89. Also note his "veneration for . . . old names" in *L&J,* 5:367.

11

The Pastoral Moment

We left Blonay with regret, and not without lingering some time on its terrace, a spot in which retirement is better blended with a bird's eye view of men and their haunts, than any other I know. One is neither in nor out of this world at such a spot; near enough to enjoy its beauties, and yet so remote as to escape its blemishes.

Sketches of Switzerland, Part 2

The pastoral moment in Cooper's fiction occurs when the eye takes possession of its rightful holdings. We witness such a moment in *Home as Found* as John Effingham leads his family (returning from Europe) to "a small open spot in a forest, and on the verge of a precipitous mountain." It is appropriate that this site, visited earlier in history by the characters in *The Pioneers*, is called "the Vision," for such clearings provide the ideal setting for the eye's gathering of its possessions.

John Effingham has "prepared this scene for his friends" with care, in order to insure their "surprise" and "delight," and their "bursts of pleasure" remind us of Natty Bumppo's initial response to this same landscape in *The Deerslayer*. Like Natty, who views the scene from a similar clearing, the Effinghams experience a sudden feeling of location. Yet their response is, in one sense, fuller than Leatherstocking's, for what they have located is the landscape of home: " 'Now do I know where we are,' exclaimed Eve, clasping her hands in rapture—'this is the "Vision," and yonder, indeed, is our blessed home' " (145). The panoramic description of "home" is worth citing at some length:

Hundreds of feet beneath them, directly in front, and stretching leagues to the right, was a lake embedded in woods and hills. On the side next the travellers a fringe of forest broke the line of water; tree tops that intercepted the view of the shores; and on the other, high broken hills, or low mountains rather, that were covered with farms, beautifully relieved by patches of wood, in a way to resemble the scenery of a vast park or a royal pleasure-ground, limited the landscape. High valleys lay among these uplands, and in every direction comfortable dwellings dotted the fields. The dark hues of the evergreens, with which all the heights near the water were shaded, were in soft contrast to the livelier green of the other foliage, while the meadows and pastures were luxuriant with a verdure unsurpassed by that of England. Bays and points added to the exquisite outline of the glassy lake on this shore, while one of the former withdrew towards the north-west, in a way to leave the eye doubtful whether it was the termination of the transparent sheet or not. Towards the south, bold, varied, but cultivated hills, also bounded the view, all teeming with the fruits of human labor, and yet all relieved by pieces of wood in the way already mentioned, so as to give the entire region the character of park scenery. A wide, deep, even valley commenced at the southern end of the lake, or nearly opposite to the stand of our travellers, and stretched away south, until concealed by a curvature in the ranges of the mountains. . . .

. . . At the northern termination of this lovely valley, and immediately on the margin of the lake, lay the village of Templeton, immediately under the eyes of the party. [146–47]

Here is Cooper's original geography, his own landscape of home, for Templeton is a barely altered version of Cooperstown. This is the central place of the writer's imagination, the world founded by his father and defended from attack by Cooper himself. As he renders it here, even the landscape helps him to perform this protective function. Just as the mountains in *The Deerslayer* serve as "barriers to exclude the outer world," the hills in *Home as Found* "limited" and "bounded the view."

This "lovely valley" provided Cooper with the visual schema for all his "island" settings, from the valley of the Wish-ton-Wish to the park-like oak openings. As "the eyes of the party" scan the panorama, the various aspects of the writer's pastoral vision are tallied. At the center is the "lake embedded in woods and hills," and this treasure radiates its beauty outward to the neatly arranged fields and woodlands. The surrounding hills take on added value because of their resemblance to European "park scenery," and the central portion of the description reads very much like a selection from Cooper's travel books on Switzerland.

The moment of repossession of this valued landscape belongs as much to Cooper as it does to the fictional Effinghams. Yet the whole point of *Home as Found* is to demonstrate that this moment is illusory. The distant view of the landscape hides from the characters "the ravages man had committed in that noble forest" (144), ravages all too apparent upon a closer inspection. Sadly, the home found by the Effinghams has suffered the spoliation of time. For the "lovely valley" has been invaded by the likes of Aristabulus Bragg, a character who violates boundaries of all kinds (social, legal, geographical). The pastoral moment, as it occurs in this novel, is an isolated and purely visual experience. Cooper paints this beautiful landscape only in order to show how much the impressive "far view" contrasts with the disappointing "near view." Like several of his other didactic novels, *Home as Found* makes a far too pointed contrast between these views, and the beauty of nature becomes merely a weapon in the writer's arsenal against change.

But as we know, there were times in Cooper's career when he was capable of creating a true island experience in his fiction. In such books, the pastoral moment is prolonged, sustained, to embrace the entire world of the novel. When this happens, the novel itself becomes the possession, a self-contained reverie, or "cosmos," which preserves its value in art even when the reality it represents has been hopelessly lost. This dilation of the pastoral vision makes the distant view proximate and vital and puts us in touch with Cooper's deepest reserves of imagination. As we have seen, *The Deerslayer* and *Satanstoe* are two such books, books which traditional criticism has categorized, respectively, as a forest romance and a social novel. Yet both obey the same impulse, basic to all pastoral literature, the impulse to return to a simpler and more beautiful past associated with childhood.

In *Miles Wallingford*, as in *Satanstoe*, we witness the actions of a young man through the perspective of "an old fellow, whose thoughts revert to the happier scenes of youth with a species of dotage" (440). For our purposes, the key word in this phrase is "scenes," because Cooper's return to youth is accomplished by the making of a picture. His pastoral novels not only contain many lovely scenes; they are themselves scenes, "pictures" of a suspended, idyllic moment. In this way, Cooper recaptures the past with the eye. But as we saw earlier, his act of possession of the pastoral landscape is different from Emerson's. The operation of the Emersonian transparent eyeball is characterized by process; it brings about the organic transformation of the self through the motion of seeing. Cooper's eye, on the other hand, works to render the world still, even static—to frame and hold the landscape in a state of permanence. It is the difference between "seen" (process) and "scene" (stasis).

In one of his travel books, Cooper tells of the "poetical and good" effects of taking "a broad view of the earth" from a position of great elevation:

> In boyhood, my feeling was ever to fly from such places, in order to cull the beauties by again approaching them; but, as life glides away, I find the desire to recede increase, as if I would reduce the whole earth to a picture in a camera obscura, in which the outlines and general beauties are

embraced, while the disgusting details are diminished to atoms.[1]

This passage suggests the preciousness of the distant view for Cooper, and also indicates how precarious the experience of aesthetic rapture was for him. Perhaps his childhood wish to "fly from such places" so as to reexperience the joy of the first impression implicitly expresses a sense of the precariousness of childhood itself. But the passage can also be read as a program for Cooper's pastoral novels, because what they accomplish is a *holding* of the beautiful first impression ("hold" in the double sense of poise and possess). *The Deerslayer* is a result of Cooper's "desire to recede" and to "embrace" a landscape of timeless beauty.

Nature viewed from a point of great elevation becomes motionless. The viewer, no longer within the landscape, can control it with the eye; he can select and frame a scene. The solitude of a mountaintop allows Cooper the "composure" to fully possess his world, to make it still. And from the perspective of literal and moral elevation, he can ignore the "disgusting details." (For Cooper, the disgusting details were a part of objective reality, but the second impression may have been spoiled for him by the surfacing of images of "difficulty" from his interior landscape.) A novel like *The Deerslayer* takes just such a distant view, not only of space but also of time. In this way, Cooper can "diminish" the "disgusting details" of the historical foreground and preserve permanently the purity and joy of the first impression.

It is important to notice that Cooper diminishes rather than excludes the disgusting details. Traditionally, pastoral literature enacts a return from complexity (the city) to simplicity (the country), a return which offers an escape from greed and violence. But Cooper's pastoral "picture" does not exclude

1. *Excursions in Italy*, p. 155. For a discussion of such scenes as retreats, see Collins, "Cooper and the American Dream," pp. 89–90.

greed and violence; it contains them. For all that Thomas Hutter would do, he is powerless to act out his destructive impulses. To paraphrase William Empson's formula, Cooper's pastoral overwhelms the complex with the simple.[2]

In his work, the pastoral condition is established by framing the picture with an impenetrable boundary, a boundary marked off by time; past and *pastoral* are inextricably related. As long as the frame remains unbroken, the illusion of permanence is sustained, regardless of what individual acts of greed and violence take place within the picture. In a novel like *The Crater*, Cooper himself breaks the frame and allows the forces of the "outside" to penetrate his Eden, to generate the fatal dynamics of history. But in pastoral novels such as *The Deerslayer*, the frame remains unbroken. The Hurons who attack the castle, for example, are a relatively small party, which has become detached from the main force. The war in which they have taken part is distant, a situation completely unlike *The Last of the Mohicans*, where Cooper plunges us directly into the center of military conflict. Similarly, the indiscriminate killing of the Indians by soldiers from the fort, while bloody, mindless, and saddening, is not comparable to the massive violence depicted in the earlier-written work. The scene occurs very late in *The Deerslayer* and is a somewhat arbitrary device which enables Cooper to save his principal characters from otherwise certain death (as we have seen, there is nothing arbitrary about such scenes in *The Last of the Mohicans*). This is but a momentary interruption of the novel's primary movement, not its culmination. The troops, who arrive just in time to rescue Leatherstocking and his companions from the Hurons, make their sudden entrance from far "outside" the novel's stage and depart just as quickly as they had arrived. Soon the Glimmerglass is restored to a state of uninterrupted solitude.

2. Empson defines "the pastoral process" as one of "putting the complex into the simple" (*Some Versions of Pastoral*, p. 22).

One of the functions of the scene is to predict the military violence and destruction that European "engines of war" will bring on a much larger scale in the later period represented in *The Last of the Mohicans*. But in *The Deerslayer* a magnificent landscape fully "contains" the violence of both Indian and European warfare. As in the first two paintings of *The Course of Empire* ("The Savage State" and "The Arcadian State"), the natural setting utterly overwhelms the human, and the development of empire is held in the distant future, a picture to be painted within an entirely different frame.

Edmund Wilson calls *The Deerslayer* "a dream full of danger."[3] There is danger, to be sure, but, as Wilson implies, it is danger *within* a dream. Contained by the dream, it does not disturb the integrity of the pastoral moment but works instead to electrify it, saving it from placidity. (The same can be said of *The Water Witch*, a nautical romance which dramatizes violent action but sustains an idyllic quality.) There is nothing contradictory about the juxtaposition of danger and dream in Cooper's work. Acute danger, in fact, is the context for the most intense of island experiences in his novels. Corny Littlepage, stranded with Anneke Mordaunt in the middle of a terrifying upheaval of ice on the Hudson, records his reaction: "I had a wild but sweet consolation in thus finding myself, as it might be, cut off from all the rest of my kind, in the midst of that scene of gloom and desolation, alone with Anneke Mordaunt" (268). "Moments like those," Corny says, "make one alive to all the affections, and strip off every covering that habit, or the dissembling of our manners is so apt to throw over the feelings. I believe I both spoke and acted toward Anneke, as one would cling to, or address the being dearest to him in the world, for the next few minutes" (269). Danger in Cooper's world, then, can bring intimacy, a throwing off of conventions imposed by the civilized world. And such simplicity and openness of response are at the heart of pastoral experience.

3. *The Shock of Recognition,* p. 581.

Cooper's critical responses indicate he did not fully understand the dynamics of his own pastoral art; for example, he thought *The Chainbearer* "a more interesting book than Satanstoe" (*L&J*, 5: 107). And he would not have been pleased to hear that his finest works are those in which he creates an illusion. As Richard Chase has written, Cooper regarded "his novels as public acts"[4] and wished for them public, reformist functions. For him, the act of purely aesthetic appropriation of the landscape was not, as it was for Emerson, an inherently superior mode. Rather, it became a substitute means of possession. The canopy he most desperately wanted to preserve was the one that covers the family pew in *The Redskins*, but this canopy—the principal symbol in the novel of the special status of the Littlepage family—is "destroyed" (454) by the rapacious forces of the "outside." For this reason, he created—imaginatively inhabited—another protected space, one formed by the canopy of forest and sky. Finding that he could not trust man, Cooper chose instead to trust nature.

But the fact that nature served him as a substitute does not make Cooper's pastoral vision a secondary experience for us. For in the act of substituting, he generalizes, makes universal, what otherwise would have been a narrow response. Indeed, in many of the social novels, such narrowness of response is precisely what we feel. But deflected from his immediate social concerns, Cooper's vision takes on the quality, as Lawrence recognized, of a "yearning myth."[5] The sense of loss remains, but it works to charge the writer's vision with an intense, precarious beauty, and when he achieves such a genuine transformation of anxiety into art, the quality of immediate threat diminishes and a true island experience emerges.

The success of a book like *The Deerslayer* can be accounted for in somewhat the same way as Frederick Crews accounts for the success of *The Scarlet Letter*. In that novel, Crews argues, "Hawthorne has succeeded for once in containing his anxieties almost entirely within an ironic portrait of the mind" which

---

4. *The American Novel and Its Tradition*, p. 47.
5. *Studies in Classic American Literature*, p. 51.

allows him to keep his obsessions "better concealed from view."[6] If we strike the word "ironic" and give the word "portrait" a more literal (pictorial) meaning than Crews intends, then this explanation applies nicely to Cooper's pastoral novels. When the pictorial aspects of his art dominate his vision (when he allows this to happen), Cooper's voice relaxes; the petulant, often strident, tone of the social novels diminishes, and we sense the writer becoming absorbed (himself "contained") by the picture.

As I have suggested, Cooper never fully identified his own artistic strengths, and because of this only a few of his works—those written out of particularly favorable circumstances—possess the beauty and power of *The Deerslayer*. But this explanation is not sufficient. I think we might well ask whether any writer could have deliberately created the idyllic quality of such a novel, for pastoral is an inherently precarious condition defined by the tensions it exhibits.[7] It may be that the idyllic moment of *The Deerslayer* could only have resulted from the temporary abatement of massive tensions, tensions such as we know Cooper experienced. Just as the clearing—the protected "inside"—is defined by its relationship to the threatening "outside," pastoral can only exist in contrast to complexity or "difficulty."

And childhood, the source of Cooper's pastoral vision, is itself a precarious condition. Although it is remembered in reverie as a timeless, immobile state of being, it is in reality a very fragile moment in human development. As Anna Freud writes, childhood is a state during which "inner balance [is] achieved, [and] although characteristic for each individual and precious to him, is preliminary only and precarious."[8] To the extent that pastoral art grows out of childhood reverie, it is certain to carry the sense of a world doomed to loss. And this is precisely the quality of Cooper's pastoral novels.

6. *The Sins of the Fathers*, pp. 135, 268.
7. See Herbert Lindenberger, who discusses "island experiences" in European pastoral literature ("The Idyllic Moment," passim).
8. "Adolescence," p. 264.

In another way, too, pastoral is a fragile condition. As a literary form, it is difficult to sustain. On the one hand, it easily becomes sentimental and, on the other, it turns self-conscious and ironic. Cooper's success as a pastoral artist can be accounted for, perhaps, by the fact that his concern for realism prevented sentimentality while his essential naiveté closed off the ironic response. In any case, in those works in which he allows his rich imagination to work freely, he performs for us that function which Bachelard says is the work of the great writer: "We ask great writers to transmit their reveries to us, confirm us in our reveries and thus permit us to live in our reimagined past."[9]

Yet his work does more than this. For the past he allows us to reexperience is not only our own but also the nation's. The German critic Schiller wisely expanded the definition of pastoral beyond all specific literary forms and identified it as a state of mind, one which he said was universal: "All people who possess a history have a paradise, a state of innocence, a golden age; indeed, every human being has his paradise, his golden age, which he remembers with enthusiasm to the degree that he possesses something of the poetical in his nature."[10] Cooper charges the nation's golden age with the reverie of his own remembered childhood and thereby accomplishes a vital intersection of public and private worlds. It is in this way that he created America's youth and made available to us what Lawrence called the "myth of America."[11]

I have suggested that the peculiar appeal of a book like *The Deerslayer* could only have come from Cooper's unique sensibility. Yet it may also be true that it could only have been written in the first half of the nineteenth century, in a period when Americans possessed a vital sense of the pastoral. It was still possible for Cooper, as it may not have been for any writer coming of age after the massive dislocations caused by the Civil

9. *The Poetics of Reverie*, p. 120.

10. Johann Friedrich von Schiller, *Werke*, 8:161; cited and translated by Lindenberger in "The Idyllic Moment," p. 347.

11. *Studies in Classic American Literature*, p. 54.

War, to find in the nation's immediate past an analogue for
one's own growing up. Later, when that analogy breaks down,
the sense of the pastoral remains—it has permanent status in
the human imagination—but it becomes detached and distant,
a subject for nostalgia. Cooper may have been the last of our
great writers to locate the pastoral so firmly in our common
history, to give it such an identifiable "place" in the imagination.

But his fiction takes us back even farther into our common
past, for, as we have seen, he renders America's golden age
with the imagery of an older landscape. His woods are defined
as much by European parks and gardens as they are by the
actual terrain of the American continent. Because of this, they
have very little regional identification; they are not particular
woods but classic woods—a landscape of the mind. As a child
Cooper memorized large portions of Vergil's *Eclogues*, a fact
which reminds us that his Arcadia draws as much of its power
from European sources as it does from his knowledge of the
American wilderness. The popular conception of him as a
frontier writer (one shared by many critics) needs to be carefully reconsidered and qualified. The expansive continent ex-
cited Cooper's imagination, yet his basic impulse was not toward expansion but toward consolidation.[12] As a social thinker
he wanted the American population to be clustered in major
centers in the East, not dispersed over the entire country. And
as an artist, his deepest wish was to see the American landscape
as organized, structured space.

By visualizing America in this way, Cooper gives to the
American pastoral a quality of permanence. He thereby se-
cures an ideal essential to our culture, a culture whose destiny is
predicated on the possibilities of life in nature. Readers of all
generations since Cooper's have undoubtedly found this ideal
in his books, but for our own time he offers a particularly
poignant aspect of the usable past. For if the American pastoral

12. Even *The Prairie*, as Joel Porte has shown, dramatizes Cooper's wish to
merge European and American values (*The Romance in America*, pp. 41–52).

had been eroded by the second half of the nineteenth century, then surely it has been almost lost for us. Today, more than ever, we feel the need to be inspired by a timeless vision of simplicity and childhood wonder. As our own environment becomes increasingly threatened by spoliation and as our own "difficulty" becomes more acute, we can turn to Cooper to recover, perhaps to cultivate for the first time, a sense of the pastoral.

Works Cited

Addison, Joseph. *The Spectator*. Edited by G. Gregory Smith. Vol. 6. New York, 1898.

Arnheim, Rudolf. *Art and Visual Perception: A Psychology of the Creative Eye*. Berkeley, 1954.

Bachelard, Gaston. *On Poetic Imagination and Reverie: Selections from the Works of Gaston Bachelard*. Edited and translated by Colette Gaudin. New York, 1971.

———. *The Poetics of Reverie: Childhood, Language, and the Cosmos*. Translated by Daniel Russell. Boston, 1969.

———. *The Poetics of Space*. Translated by Maria Jolas. Boston, 1964.

———. *The Psychoanalysis of Fire*. Translated by Alan C. M. Ross. Boston, 1964.

Balzac, Honoré de. "Lettres sur la littérature." *Oeuvres Complètes*, 23: 584–90. Paris, 1869–79.

Baym, Nina. "The Women of Cooper's Leatherstocking Tales." *American Quarterly* 23 (December 1971): 696–709.

Beard, James F. "Afterword." *The Last of the Mohicans*. New York, 1962.

———. "Cooper and His Artistic Contemporaries." *New York History* 35 (1954): 480–95.

———. "James Fenimore Cooper." In *Fifteen American Authors before 1900: Bibliographic Essays on Research and Criticism*. Edited by Robert A. Rees and Earl N. Harbert. Madison, Wis., 1971.

Bewley, Marius. *The Eccentric Design: Form in the Classic American Novel*. New York, 1963.

Black Elk Speaks: Being the Life Story of a Holy Man of the Oglala Sioux. As told through John G. Neihardt. New York, 1932.

Blair, Hugh. *Lectures on Rhetoric and Belles Lettres*. Vol. 2. Dublin, 1783.

Brady, Charles A. "Myth-Maker and Christian Romancer." In

American Classics Reconsidered: A Christian Appraisal, edited by Harold C. Gardiner, S.J., pp. 59–97. New York, 1958.

Brooks, Van Wyck. *The Ordeal of Mark Twain.* New York, 1920.

Brown, Charles Brockden. *Edgar Huntly; or, Memoirs of a Sleep-Walker.* Port Washington, N.Y., 1887.

Brown, Norman O. *Love's Body.* New York, 1966.

Brownell, William C. *American Prose Masters: Cooper, Hawthorne, Emerson, Poe, Lowell, Henry James.* Edited by Howard Mumford Jones. Cambridge, Mass., 1963.

Callow, James T. *Kindred Spirits: Knickerbocker Writers and American Artists, 1807–1855.* Chapel Hill, N.C., 1967.

Campbell, Joseph. *The Hero with a Thousand Faces.* Princeton, 1949.

Charvat, William. *The Origins of American Critical Thought: 1810–1835.* Philadelphia, 1936.

Chase, Richard. *The American Novel and Its Tradition.* Garden City, N.Y., 1957.

Clavel, Marcel. *Fenimore Cooper: Sa vie et son œuvre: La Jeunesse (1789–1826).* Aix-en-Provence, 1938.

Clemens, Samuel L. "Fenimore Cooper's Literary Offenses." *The Writings of Mark Twain: Author's National Edition.* Vol. 22. New York, 1899.

Cobb, Edith. "The Ecology of Imagination in Childhood." *Daedalus: Journal of the American Academy of Arts and Sciences* 88 (Summer 1959): 537–48.

Cole, Thomas. "Essay on American Scenery." *The American Monthly Magazine* 1 (January 1836): 1–12.

Collins, Frank M. "Cooper and the American Dream." *PMLA* 81 (March 1966): 79–94.

Cooper, James Fenimore. "American and European Scenery Compared." In *The Home Book of the Picturesque; or, American Scenery, Art, and Literature.* New York, 1851.

———. *The American Democrat.* Edited by George Dekker and Larry Johnson. Baltimore, 1969.

———. *Cooper's Novels.* 32 vols. Illustrated from drawings by F. O. C. Darley. New York, 1859–61.

————. *Early Critical Essays: 1820–1822.* Edited by James F. Beard. Gainesville, Fla., 1955.

————. *Excursions in Italy.* Paris, 1838.

————. *Gleanings in Europe: England.* 2 vols. Philadelphia, 1837.

————. *Gleanings in Europe: France.* Edited by Robert E. Spiller. New York, 1928.

————. *The Last of the Mohicans; A Narrative of 1757.* Philadelphia, 1826.

————. *The Letters and Journals of James Fenimore Cooper.* Edited by James F. Beard. 6 vols. Cambridge, Mass., 1960, 1964, 1968.

————. *Notions of the Americans Picked Up by a Traveling Bachelor.* Edited by Robert E. Spiller. 2 vols. New York, 1963.

————. *Sketches of Switzerland.* Part 1. 2 vols. Philadelphia, 1836.

————. *Sketches of Switzerland.* Part 2. 2 vols. Philadelphia, 1836.

Cooper, James Fenimore [the novelist's grandson]. *The Legends and Traditions of a Northern Country.* New York, 1921.

Cooper, Susan Fenimore. *Pages and Pictures from the Writings of James Fenimore Cooper, with Notes.* New York, 1861.

Crews, Frederick. *The Sins of the Fathers: Hawthorne's Psychological Themes.* New York, 1966.

Darnell, Donald. "Uncas as Hero: The *Ubi Sunt* Formula in *The Last of the Mohicans.*" *American Literature* 37 (November 1965): 259–66.

Davie, Donald. *The Heyday of Sir Walter Scott.* London, 1961.

Dekker, George. *James Fenimore Cooper the Novelist.* London, 1967.

Dryden, Edgar A. "History and Progress: Some Implications of Form in Cooper's Littlepage Novels." *Nineteenth-Century Fiction* 26 (June 1971): 49–64.

Du Bos, Charles. "On the 'Inner Environment' in the Work of Flaubert." In *Madame Bovary: Backgrounds and Sources, Essays in Criticism,* edited and translated by Paul de Man, pp. 360–71. New York, 1965. Originally published in *Approximations I.* Paris, 1922.

Eliade, Mircea. *The Myth of the Eternal Return; or, Cosmos and History*. Translated by Willard R. Trask. Princeton, 1959.

————. *The Sacred and the Profane: The Nature of Religion*. Translated by Willard R. Trask. New York, 1959.

Ellis, David M. "The Coopers and New York State Landholding Systems." *New York History* 35 (1954): 412–22.

Emerson, Ralph Waldo. *The Collected Works of Ralph Waldo Emerson*. Vol. 1. Edited by Alfred R. Ferguson. Cambridge, Mass., 1971.

Empson, William. *Some Versions of Pastoral*. New York, 1968.

Erikson, Erik H. *Childhood and Society*. 2nd Edition. New York, 1963.

Feidelson, Charles, Jr. *Symbolism and American Literature*. Chicago, 1953.

Fiedler, Leslie A. *Love and Death in the American Novel*. New York, 1966.

Foerster, Norman. *Nature in American Literature: Studies in the Modern View of Nature*. New York, 1958.

French, David P. "James Fenimore Cooper and Fort William Henry." *American Literature* 32 (March 1960): 28–38.

Freud, Anna. "Adolescence." *The Psychoanalytic Study of the Child* 13 (1958): 255–78.

Freud, Sigmund. *A General Introduction to Psycho-Analysis: A Course of Twenty-Eight Lectures Delivered at the University of Vienna*. Translated by Joan Riviere. New York, 1935.

Frye, Northrop. *Anatomy of Criticism: Four Essays*. Princeton, 1957.

Fuller, Margaret. *The Writings of Margaret Fuller*. Edited by Mason Wade. New York, 1941.

Fussell, Edwin. *Frontier: American Literature and the American West*. Princeton, 1965.

Genette, Gerard. "Time and Narrative in *A la recherche du temps perdu*." In *Aspects of Narrative: Selected Papers from the English Institute*, edited by J. Hillis Miller, pp. 93–118. New York, 1971.

Gombrich, E. H. *Art and Illusion: A Study in the Psychology of Pictorial Representation*. 4th Edition. Princeton, 1972.

————. *Meditations on a Hobby Horse and Other Essays on the Theory of Art*. London, 1963.

Goodman, Paul. *The Empire City*. Indianapolis, 1959.

Grigson, Geoffrey. "The Room Outdoors." *Landscape* 4 (1954–55): 25–29.

Grossman, James. *James Fenimore Cooper*. New York, 1949.

Hagstrum, Jean. *The Sister Arts: The Tradition of Literary Pictorialism and English Poetry from Dryden to Gray*. Chicago, 1958.

Hale, Edward Everett, Jr. "American Scenery in Cooper's Novels." *Sewanee Review* 18 (1910): 317–32.

Hall, Edward T. *The Hidden Dimension*. New York, 1969.

————. *The Silent Language*. Garden City, N.Y., 1959.

Heckewelder, John. *History, Manners, and Customs of the Indian Nations Who Once Inhabited Pennsylvania and the Neighboring States*. [*Memoirs of the Historical Society of Pennsylvania*. Vol. 12.] Philadelphia, 1876; Rpt. 1971. Originally published 1819.

Henderson, Harry B., 3rd. *Versions of the Past: The Historical Imagination in American Fiction*. New York, 1974.

Henderson, Joseph L. *Thresholds of Initiation*. Middletown, Conn., 1967.

House, Kay S. *Cooper's Americans*. Columbus, 1965.

Howard, David. "James Fenimore Cooper's *Leatherstocking Tales*: 'without a cross.' " In *Tradition and Tolerance in Nineteenth-Century Fiction: Critical Essays on Some English and American Novels*. Edited by David Howard, John Lucas, John Goode. New York, 1967.

Iser, Wolfgang. "Indeterminacy and the Reader's Response in Prose Fiction." In *Aspects of Narrative: Selected Papers from the English Institute*, edited by J. Hillis Miller, pp. 1–45. New York, 1971.

Johnston, Kenneth R. "The Idiom of Vision." In *New Perspectives on Coleridge and Wordsworth: Selected Papers from the English Institute*, edited by Geoffrey H. Hartman, pp. 1–39. New York, 1972.

Jones, Howard Mumford. "Prose and Pictures: James Fenimore Cooper." *Tulane Studies in English* 3 (1952): 133–54.

Kaul, A. N. *The American Vision: Actual and Ideal Society in Nineteenth-Century Fiction*. New Haven, 1963.

Kiely, Robert. *Robert Louis Stevenson and the Fiction of Adventure*. Cambridge, Mass., 1964.

Kolodny, Annette. *The Lay of the Land: Metaphor as Experience and History in American Life and Letters*. Chapel Hill, N.C., 1975.

Lawrence, D. H. *Studies in Classic American Literature*. New York, 1961.

————. *The Symbolic Meaning: The Uncollected Versions of "Studies in Classic American Literature."* Edited by Armin Arnold. Fontwell, England, 1961.

Lévi-Strauss, Claude. *Tristes Tropiques: An Anthropological Study of Primitive Societies in Brazil*. Translated by John Russell. New York, 1972.

Lewis, R. W. B. *The American Adam: Innocence, Tragedy, and Tradition in the Nineteenth Century*. Chicago, 1955.

Lindenberger, Herbert. "The Idyllic Moment: On Pastoral and Romanticism." *College English* 34 (December 1972): 335–51.

Lynen, John. *The Design of the Present: Essays on Time and Form in American Literature*. New Haven, 1969.

Martin, Harold C. "The Development of Style in Nineteenth-Century American Fiction." In *Style in Prose Fiction: English Institute Essays, 1958,* edited by Harold C. Martin, pp. 114–41. New York, 1959.

Martin, Terence. "From the Ruins of History: *The Last of the Mohicans.*" *Novel: A Forum on Fiction* 2 (Spring 1969): 221–29.

————. *The Instructed Vision: Scottish Common Sense Philosophy and the Origins of American Fiction*. Bloomington, Ind., 1961.

Marx, Leo. *The Machine in the Garden: Technology and the Pastoral Ideal in America*. New York, 1964.

Matthiessen, F. O. *American Renaissance: Art and Expression in the Age of Emerson and Whitman*. New York, 1941.

McAleer, John J. "Biblical Analogy in the Leatherstocking Tales." *Nineteenth-Century Fiction* 17 (December 1962): 217–35.

McLuhan, Marshall, and Parker, Harley. *Through the Vanishing Point: Space in Poetry and Painting.* New York, 1968.

McWilliams, John P., Jr. *Political Justice in a Republic: James Fenimore Cooper's America.* Berkeley, 1972.

Mead, Sidney, *The Lively Experiment: The Shaping of Christianity in America.* New York, 1963.

Melville, Herman. *Moby Dick.* Edited by Harrison Hayford and Hershel Parker. New York, 1967.

Meyers, Marvin. *The Jacksonian Persuasion: Politics and Belief.* Stanford, 1960.

Miller, J. Hillis. *Thomas Hardy: Distance and Desire.* Cambridge, Mass., 1970.

Nash, Roderick. *Wilderness and the American Mind.* Revised Edition. New Haven, 1973.

Nevius, Blake. *Cooper's Landscapes: An Essay on the Picturesque Vision.* Berkeley, 1976.

Ortega y Gasset, José. "On Point of View in the Arts." *Partisan Review* 16 (August 1949): 822–36.

Paul, Sherman. *Emerson's Angle of Vision: Man and Nature in American Experience.* Cambridge, Mass., 1952.

Pearce, Roy Harvey. *Savagism and Civilization: A Study of the Indian and the American Mind.* Baltimore, 1965.

Peck, H. Daniel. "A Repossession of America: The Revolution in Cooper's Trilogy of Nautical Romances." *Studies in Romanticism* 15 (Fall 1976).

Philbrick, Thomas. "Cooper's *The Pioneers:* Origins and Structure." *PMLA* 79 (December 1964): 579–93.

———. "Introduction." *The Crater.* Cambridge, Mass., 1962.

———. *James Fenimore Cooper and the Development of American Sea Fiction.* Cambridge, Mass., 1961.

———. "*The Last of the Mohicans* and the Sounds of Discord." *American Literature* 43 (March 1971): 25–41.

———. "The Sources of Cooper's Knowledge of Fort William Henry." *American Literature* 36 (May 1964): 209–14.

Poirier, Richard. *A World Elsewhere: The Place of Style in American Literature.* New York, 1966.

Porte, Joel. *The Romance in America: Studies in Cooper, Poe, Hawthorne, Melville, and James.* Middletown, Conn., 1969.

Radcliffe, Ann. *The Italian.* 3 vols. London, 1811.

Raglan, Lord Fitz Roy. *The Hero: A Study in Tradition, Myth, and Drama.* New York, 1956.

Ringe, Donald A. "Cooper's *Lionel Lincoln*: The Problem of Genre." In *Long Fiction of the American Renaissance: A Symposium on Genre.* Edited by Paul McCarthy. Hartford, Conn., 1974.

————. *James Fenimore Cooper.* New Haven, 1962.

————. "James Fenimore Cooper and Thomas Cole: An Analogous Technique." *American Literature* 30 (March 1958): 26–36.

————. *The Pictorial Mode: Space and Time in the Art of Bryant, Irving, and Cooper.* Lexington, Ky., 1971.

Rosenberg, Harold. *The Tradition of the New.* New York, 1961.

Sandy, Alan F. "The Sublime, the Beautiful, and the Picturesque in the Natural Description of James Fenimore Cooper." Ph.D. dissertation, University of California, 1965.

Sanford, Charles L. *The Quest for Paradise: Europe and the American Moral Imagination.* Urbana, Ill., 1961.

Schiller, Johann Friedrich von. *Werke.* Vol. 8. Edited by Arthur Kutscher. Berlin, n.d.

Seelye, John. "Some Green Thoughts on a Green Theme." *TriQuarterly,* no. 23/24 (Winter-Spring 1972), 576–638.

Shepard, Paul. *Man in the Landscape: A Historic View of the Esthetics of Nature.* New York, 1967.

Shulenberger, Arvid. *Cooper's Theory of Fiction: His Prefaces and Their Relation to His Novels.* Lawrence, Kans., 1955.

Slotkin, Richard. *Regeneration through Violence: The Mythology of the American Frontier, 1600–1860.* Middletown, Conn., 1973.

Smith, Henry Nash. *Virgin Land: The American West as Symbol and Myth.* New York, 1950.

Snyder, Gary. *Earth House Hold: Technical Notes & Queries to Fellow Dharma Revolutionaries.* New York, 1969.

Spacks, Patricia. *The Poetry of Vision: Five Eighteenth-Century Poets.* Cambridge, Mass., 1967.

Spiller, Robert E. *Fenimore Cooper: Critic of His Times.* New York, 1931.

Spiller, Robert E., and Blackburn, Philip C. *A Descriptive Bibliography of the Writings of James Fenimore Cooper.* New York, 1934.

Tanner, Tony. "Notes for a Comparison between American and European Romanticism." *Journal of American Studies* 2 (April 1968): 83–103.

Thoreau, Henry D. *Walden.* Edited by J. Lyndon Shanley. Princeton, 1971.

Thorslev, Peter L., Jr. *The Byronic Hero: Types and Prototypes.* Minneapolis, 1962.

Tuveson, Ernest. *The Imagination as a Means of Grace: Locke and the Aesthetics of Romanticism.* Berkeley, 1960.

Watt, Ian. *The Rise of the Novel: Studies in Defoe, Richardson, and Fielding.* Berkeley, 1965.

Wilson, Edmund, ed. *The Shock of Recognition: The Development of Literature in the United States Recorded by the Men Who Made It.* New York, 1955.

Winters, Yvor. "Fenimore Cooper, or The Ruins of Time." In *In Defense of Reason.* London, 1960.

Zoellner, Robert H. "Conceptual Ambivalence in Cooper's Leatherstocking." *American Literature* 31 (January 1960): 397–420.

Index